The Family
FIGHT
Planning to Avoid It

The Family FIGHT

Planning to Avoid It

A No Nonsense Guide To Wills & Estates

BARRY FISH, B.A., B.C.L., LL.B

LES KOTZER, B.A., (HONS.), LL.B

CONTINENTAL ATLANTIC PUBLICATIONS INC.

First published in 2002
Second edition in 2003

Printed in Canada

Published by Continental Atlantic Publications Inc.
Inquiries can be made c/o
4200 Wisconsin Ave., N.W.
PMB #106-229
Washington D.C.
U.S.A. 20016-2143

Tel: 1-888-965-1500
www.familyfight.com

ISBN 0-9683513-6-0

A WORD ABOUT THE AUTHORS

Both Barry M. Fish and Les Kotzer are Wills and Estates lawyers who have been practicing for many years. Barry commenced practicing in 1973 and Les commenced in 1989. Les graduated law school as a dean's honour roll student. Both Les and Barry have been featured in numerous newspaper and magazine articles and have appeared as guests on many radio and television shows, where they have spoken generally on this subject and specifically about estate planning with a view to keeping the family together. They are often invited to give seminars and talks to the public and to various trade and professional organizations. Their previous book was entitled "Speaking of Wills: What You Should Know From A Lawyer's Perspective".

FOREWORD

The focus of this book is estate planning with a view to avoiding family fighting. By way of an introduction, let us briefly highlight some of the issues which we will be discussing. We will begin with an introduction to two of the most important documents you will ever sign during your life. These documents consist firstly of the Durable Power of Attorney for Property, which will enable you to appoint someone you trust to look after your financial affairs in the event that you become incapable of making financial decisions for yourself; secondly, the Durable Power of Attorney for Health Care which enables you to appoint someone you trust to make personal and health care decisions for you in the event that, by reason of your incapacity, you become unable to do so for yourself. We will be discussing issues to think about regarding these documents and specifically, what to think about when you set them up so that you will avoid or at least minimize family fights in the event of your incapacity.

After having dealt with the importance of Power of Attorney documents which protect you during your lifetime, we then turn to what happens after your death. We will be introducing you to the importance of a Will and the problems which are likely to result if you die without having one. We will then examine the careful thought that must be devoted to the various components of your Will in order to avoid fighting within your family after you die. Our discussion regarding the components of your Will is going to extend to a number of issues including executors, dealing with the personal items which you treasure, guardianship of your young children and a number of other important matters.

The discussion will then pass to various estate planning considerations. Within this discussion you will read about the difference between giving your assets outright under your Will as opposed to setting up a trust in your Will. Just how much freedom do you really have, to dispose of your assets in your Will? Can you cut out your spouse? Can you cut out a child? You will read about the answers to such questions. Your attention will be drawn to methods of giving your property to others without using your Will, such as in the case of joint ownership of property. You will see how the joint ownership mechanism works.

You will see how important it becomes to review your Will if you wish to avoid family disputes. We will examine the important implications of marriage, separation and divorce. Before leaving the subject of estate planning considerations, we will touch upon the dangers of homemade Wills and the dangers of changing your Will without professional advice.

We will focus upon organizing your affairs so that your family will not be left confused and unprepared in the event of your unexpected incapacity or death.

We will then examine how fights can occur as a result of inappropriate assumptions which people commonly make in planning their estates.

Under the heading of inheriting turmoil you will see some real life examples of just how wrong things have gone for some families.

We will then provide suggestions and strategies to consider when you wish to accomplish a number of things such as cutting out a child, providing a fair and reasonable benefit to a caregiving child, avoiding inadvertent inequality among those who are to benefit from your estate, and dealing with the family home and the family business.

We are dedicating this book to the loving memories of Les' mother Rose, and Barry's father Abe, each of whom were a major source of inspiration for the creation of this work. We are also dedicating this book to our loving families, and thank them for their patience and support during the long hours which we spent in preparing our book.

TABLE OF CONTENTS

INTRODUCTION

We all like to think that we are going to be healthy and will live forever. However, the facts of life do not support this kind of a wish and there is always a risk that we may suffer from a debilitating disease, or that we might be involved in a major accident, the result of which may leave us incapacitated. The overall fact is that one day all of us will die. There are consequences that we have no choice but to address which arise from all of these considerations. Firstly, if you lose your mental capacity to the extent that you can no longer look after your financial affairs, who is going to pay your bills, look after your bank accounts, your home, your mutual funds and other investments? Secondly, if the degree of your incapacity is such that you are unable to make medical and personal care decisions for yourself, who will make those decisions for you? Thirdly, when you are no longer living, who is going to look after your estate, who will inherit your assets and who will take care of your minor children? In all of these situations, how can you prevent your family from fighting? These are issues that all of us have to think about. It is important that we plan ahead.

Planning ahead can often prevent, or at least minimize the risk of family fighting. Planning ahead can avoid costly court actions and it can ease the burden on your loved ones, if and when tragedy strikes. The key is to plan ahead while you are able to do so. This will allow you to take advantage of the various planning strategies that the law allows.

Among such strategies you will find your ability to appoint someone to look after your financial affairs during your lifetime in the event that you lose your capacity to do so. Similarly you will find the ability to appoint someone to look after your health and personal care matters during your lifetime if you lose your capacity to make those kinds of decisions. Of course you will find that the law allows you to make a Will, which puts someone in charge of the process of protecting your estate for the benefit of your loved ones after your death, and then effecting a distribution of your assets in accordance with your wishes.

Unfortunately, far too many people procrastinate in their planning, for a variety of reasons. Perhaps some people may feel that the planning effort presents an insurmountable burden to them, or that the process they are being asked to go through contains too many terms which are not familiar to them. Let us get a feel for some of the terms which may be causing difficulties:

- Durable Power of Attorney for Property;
- Durable Power of Attorney for Health Care;
- Living Will;
- Will;
- Codicil;
- Executor;
- Beneficiary;
- Guardian;
- Joint Tenancy;
- Trust.

As foreign as some of these terms may sound, understanding them is essential because if you get sick or die with no plan in place, your family will be at risk of a fight or in the worst of cases, a family war. Accordingly, understanding these terms is essential to your efforts to avoid these risks.

We have made reference to "planning ahead". From a professional point of view, this is often referred to as estate planning.

Our book is intended to provide you with valuable information, based upon our years of experience. Our goal is to raise issues to think about and questions to ask your professional advisor regarding your estate planning. Within this broad and complicated area of the law, there are many focal points, one of which is the avoidance of family conflict. In order to achieve this end, we will examine the various elements of estate planning and we will suggest strategies which you might consider utilizing in order to keep harmony within your family.

Unfortunately, many people pass on or become incapacitated before organizing their affairs. Without proper organization your assets could go unnoticed or become lost and your loved ones may not benefit from your years of hard work. Accordingly, we are devoting considerable attention to the organizational aspect of estate planning and you will read about some organizational strategies which can ease the burden imposed upon your loved ones in managing your affairs in the event you become incapacitated or in the event that you pass away.

It is easy to say "I won't be here to worry about it", but if you look at your loving family sitting together with you for Thanksgiving dinner, laughing with each other, you should think about the importance of proper estate planning as a means of maintaining the cohesiveness of your family. Quite often an unorganized or improperly prepared estate plan can melt the glue that holds a family together.

THE DURABLE POWER OF ATTORNEY FOR PROPERTY

Let us begin by discussing the Durable Power of Attorney for Property. This important estate planning document allows you to appoint someone you trust to act on your behalf to look after your financial affairs in the event you become incapable of doing so yourself.

Many of us take our mental capacity for granted. As long as we are mentally capable, we can refinance or sell our homes, sign contracts, pay our bills, deal with our investments and make many other financial decisions. However, if we were to lose our mental capacity due to an accident or illness, it would become extremely difficult and inconvenient to deal with all of these matters in an orderly manner. This is why it is so important to have a legally enforceable Durable Power of Attorney for Property. This document will allow the person or persons appointed on the document to deal with all of these financial matters, if and when we become incapable of looking after these matters ourselves.

A few years ago a financial planner came to our office. She told us that she had been advising many of her young clients not to worry too much about this area of the law because, according to the reasoning of this financial planner, those young clients were healthy and could easily look after their own financial affairs. According to this financial planner, a Durable Power of Attorney for Property was something elderly people had to consider. She felt that her younger clients had plenty of time to consider this matter. However, in our meeting with her, we told her that her reasoning contained one very significant oversight: even though a young person may be healthy today and fully able to look after his or her financial affairs, no one knows whether a sudden illness or an unexpected stroke, or an unforeseen traffic accident or sports accident will occur. If any of these events occur, a financial nightmare can await the families of those who are unprepared.

When you are young and healthy you tend to think that if for any reason you are going to experience mental incapacity, it will not happen overnight and you should have lots of warning signs. This is exactly what the financial  planner we just spoke about was advocating to her clients. In fact, in one of the seminars at which we had spoken, a member of the audience raised this exact point. Do you know what our answer to that person was? Traffic helicopters: you may ask "What do traffic helicopters have to do with a Durable Power of Attorney for Property?" There are traffic helicopters because there are traffic jams. There are traffic jams because there are traffic accidents: sometimes terrible ones where people hit their heads against the windshield, and suffer serious injury, but do not die. A person in such a situation is very vulnerable because without a proper Durable Power of Attorney for Property, there is no one in place who can automatically step in and manage his or her financial affairs. As a result, a potential financial nightmare awaits the family.

Not all serious injuries are traffic related. A baseball bat to the temple, a bad fall in a football game, a disastrous body check in hockey, a hard ball hitting you in the back of the head or a work related injury could all create the same problem. The emergency wards are full of people who suffer such unfortunate injuries and it should be remembered that people do not necessarily die from such injuries. In fact, the injured person may live for many years.

Not all injuries will leave you mentally incapacitated, although some of them might. You may feel protected because you have done a Will. The problem is that your Will is only going to take effect when you die. A Will is of no help to you while you are alive. In our discussion we are talking about a person who is incapacitated, not dead. The scary thing is that if you own assets such as stocks, bonds, mutual funds, real estate, a business, a bank certificate or a bank account, all of these assets may be frozen in the event that you become mentally incapable, unless of course you have signed a proper Durable Power of Attorney for Property. Without such a Power of Attorney in place, someone will have to apply to a court in order to be appointed as your representative with authority to act on your behalf with regard to your financial affairs. An application of this type is time consuming, costly and may lead to family friction. For example, one family member may feel that he or she is more qualified to act on your behalf than another one. We are aware of one person who was trying to help her incapacitated aunt sell a trailer in Florida. In the end, it cost the estate of that aunt over $10,000.00 to get the court order which appointed a person with sufficient authority to sell that trailer. You might note that a trailer will not be subject to severe fluctuations in value the way a stock or mutual fund can. What if you become incapacitated and own a mutual fund or a stock or even a bond that is losing value? You could suffer a devastating loss if, as the days or weeks or months wear on, the value continues to drop. Until someone can get authority from the court to deal with those assets and sell them, your estate could be significantly reduced in value in such a situation. Once again, the good news is that with proper planning a nightmare of this sort can be avoided.

As we have already pointed out, through a Durable Power of Attorney for Property you can appoint someone you trust to act on your behalf with respect to your financial affairs, in the event you are unable to act for yourself. It is important to note that once you lose your capacity it is too late to make a Durable Power of Attorney for Property.

The law concerning the Durable Power of Attorney for Property is complicated. In order to make it easier for you to understand the complexities in this area of the law, we would like to highlight the following points:

1. The word "Attorney" in a Durable Power of Attorney does not mean that you have to appoint your lawyer. You can appoint a trusted family member or friend. Although you are giving some-one authority in this document, it does not deprive you of the ability to act on your own behalf as long as you are capable.

2. Your Will and your Durable Power of Attorney for Property are separate and distinct documents. One does not replace the other, but you are certainly allowed to appoint the same person to represent you in both your Will and your Durable Power of Attorney for Property. Your Will only takes effect after your death and your Durable Power of Attorney for Property is only effective during your life and terminates at your death.

3. On your Durable Power of Attorney for Property you can appoint one or more persons who can act on your behalf if you become incapacitated. If you appoint only one person, consider a back up to the one whom you are appointing so that someone will be able to look after your financial affairs in the event that your primary appointee dies or becomes unable or unwilling to act on your behalf. Remember that we are approaching this subject from the point of view of keeping your family together and in this context, the naming of your attorney is a very serious matter. It should not be taken lightly. For example, if you are appointing all of your children as your attorneys, you should be aware of the difference between appointing them jointly, or on the other hand, appointing them jointly and severally. If your document appoints your children jointly, it means that all decisions will have to be made by all of your named children, acting together. On the other hand, if your document appoints your children as attorneys jointly and severally, it means that one of your children, acting alone, can make a decision without the others. Your own family situation will tell you which of these choices is best for you.

4. A Power of Attorney that you may have signed at the bank for banking purposes is not the same as the Durable Power of Attorney for Property. The bank Power of Attorney may be acceptable for banking purposes, but a bank Power of Attorney may not be durable. Even if a bank Power of Attorney is durable, the fact is that a bank Power of Attorney will always be limited to the assets you have with that bank. In such circumstances, the bank Power of Attorney would not be effective with respect to your home, your condo or any other real estate in your name and in all likelihood the bank Power of Attorney would not be effective with respect to any other assets which you own, to the extent that those assets were kept outside of that particular bank.

You may find, as many people do, that it is helpful to have a bank Power of Attorney in addition to your Durable Power of Attorney for Property. However, if this is what you intend to do, be very careful to look at the wording on any documents that you are signing. What you wish to avoid is a situation where the wording on one of the Powers of Attorney accidentally revokes the other. Can you imagine what hardship would result if your Durable Power of Attorney for Property were properly in place with all of the appropriate appointments, only to be accidentally revoked by the language on your bank Power of Attorney? This would mean that the assets in your bank would be protected but that all of your other assets would not be.

5. You may find that you will want to revoke your Durable Power of Attorney for Property and of course you can always do this as long as you have your mental capacity. However, once you lose that capacity it will be too late to revoke your Durable Power of Attorney for Property. If it is your wish to indeed revoke your Durable Power of Attorney for Property you should speak to your lawyer to ensure that the revocation will be effective.

6. This subject is not only for seniors. Remember, even if you are in your twenties, and in excellent health, you run the risk that you may unexpectedly lose your mental capacity because of a motor vehicle accident or a sports accident.

7. The person whom you appoint as your attorney in your Durable Power of Attorney for Property will have the power to deal with your investments including the making of all appropriate decisions regarding those investments, and will also have the power to deposit checks, to withdraw money and to deal with various other matters including your tax matters. Be very careful about limiting the powers contained in your Durable Power of Attorney for Property. If the document is too narrow, you will leave the person you appointed to look after your financial affairs, without all of the powers he or she will require to solve the various problems which could conceivably arise pertaining to your financial situation.

One example of a problem of this sort is where a Power of Attorney is limited to banking matters. We saw this example previously. The inability to deal with non-bank assets will in all likelihood create stress for your family and could eventually lead to conflict in your family. If you have concern as to just how much power to give to your attorney, we would suggest that you consult your lawyer.

8.   The word "Property" in the phrase "Durable Power of Attorney for Property" should not be taken to mean real estate alone. Property is a word that can describe any asset, such as an automobile, a bank account, a stock or a bond.

9.   We cannot overemphasize how important it is to appoint someone whom you completely trust to represent you in a Durable Power of Attorney for Property. If you do not trust the person, do not appoint him or her. The document is very powerful and the last thing you want is for the person you appointed to take advantage of you. If you select the wrong person to serve in this capacity, you will run the risk that the person you appointed may abuse his or her position, and may take advantage of you.

10. You should be aware that there is a very onerous duty imposed upon the person you name as your attorney. That person must act in good faith on your behalf and must always put your interests first and foremost. Your attorney is always accountable for what he or she does. By all means, if you are going to appoint a person to act on your behalf as attorney, it is best to speak to such person ahead of time. Otherwise, you risk the possibility of that person rejecting the appointment just when you need him or her most of all. The person you are appointing does not necessarily have to accept that appointment. We can recall a situation where one of our clients appointed one of his children because he felt that the particular child he was appointing happened to be well suited to carry out the role of attorney. Our client omitted to communicate the appointment to his child. As events unfolded, our client became incapable and when the child was called upon to act, everyone was surprised to learn that this was the first time the child ever knew about the appointment and everyone was even more surprised when the child rejected that appointment. By way of an ending to this story, it was sad to learn that the children who were not appointed would have been more than willing to act. However, with their father now incapacitated, it was too late to name them. They related to us firstly that they were upset at having been overlooked and secondly that they were upset at having to now carry out a complex and expensive court procedure which would have easily been avoided had they been named in the first place.

11. Turning to a marriage situation, there are a couple of points to discuss. Firstly, both the husband and the wife should have their own Durable Power of Attorney for Property. It is not appropriate to rely upon one document to carry out this function for both spouses. The second point relates to a feeling of false security that many couples have. They may feel comforted because they believe that their marriage license gives them authority to act for their spouse if their spouse becomes incapable. This is a false comfort. A marriage license confers no such authority, and certainly does not replace a Durable Power of Attorney for Property.

This, for the moment, concludes our comments on Durable Powers of Attorney for Property. Let us now turn our attention to another form of Power of Attorney, which deals with health and personal care matters.

THE DURABLE POWER OF ATTORNEY FOR HEALTH CARE AND LIVING WILL

H We have seen how a Durable Power of Attorney for Property can protect you. Similarly, we should now look at the manner in which a Durable Power of Attorney for Health Care can be of assistance to you in the event that you lose your ability to make decisions regarding your health and personal care matters. Most States allow you to appoint someone who can step in and make medical or personal care decisions for you in the event that you are no longer able to do so for yourself. In view of this, we will now examine some of the issues of which you should be aware as they relate to the Durable Power of Attorney for Health Care:

1. The Durable Power of Attorney for Health Care is often referred to as a medical and personal care power of attorney.

2. State law will govern the Durable Power of Attorney for Health Care in the same manner as State law governs the Durable Power of Attorney for Property.

3. With a Durable Power of Attorney for Health Care you can ensure that someone you trust has the right to step in and make health and personal care decisions for you in the event that you become incapable of making these decisions for yourself.

4. This is often a separate and distinct document from the Durable Power of Attorney for Property, although some States may allow the two documents to be combined in one.

5. You are allowed to appoint the same person to represent you on both documents.

6. As was the case with the Durable Power of Attorney for Property, it is important to appoint someone you trust to make these very important decisions for you. In many cases, especially in a first marriage situation, one spouse will appoint the other and as an alternative, one or more of the children, in whatever combinations are appropriate for that particular family.

7. Without a Durable Power of Attorney for Health Care, your loved ones may have to get the court involved before they can make health and personal care decisions for you. This is a prime area for family stress and conflict. Without a Durable Power of Attorney for Health Care in place, you have not formally indicated who you want to make health and personal care decisions for you, if you are incapable. The court may appoint someone to act on your behalf who is simply not the person you may have named in your own document, had you prepared one. There could be a fight between two or more of your children, each of whom may bring opposing applications to the court.

Furthermore, without a Durable Power of Attorney for Health Care in place, you have not formally indicated what your specific health and personal care wishes are. This compels your loved ones to second guess your wishes and certainly this will be placing a burden upon them.

8. The person you appoint in your Durable Power of Attorney for Health Care is often called your health care agent. It is very important to discuss your wishes with your health care agent.

9. If you have three children and you are concerned that all three children would not unanimously agree with respect to decisions regarding your health and personal care matters, you can use your Durable Power of Attorney for Health Care to appoint one or more of your children whom you feel will best represent your interests in the event that you become incapable of making health and personal care decisions for yourself. The one or ones you appoint will have priority over the others with respect to these matters.

Your health care agent will have the authority to be your spokesperson, sometimes known as a patient advocate. You are the one who wishes to have as good a lifestyle as you possibly can, given your medical circumstances. The best way for this to happen is to appoint wisely. You may feel it is unfair to appoint one out of three children, but would you want all three of your children arguing in front of a doctor? You should pick a health care agent whom you feel is most dedicated to you, and you feel will be the most likely to carry out your wishes. It is not an easy job, so do not think that you are hurting someone's feelings by not appointing him or her. You should speak with all of your children and find out whether indeed they want this position as health care agent. You should also consider logistics. If you appoint all of your children, are they all able to look after you? Will they be able to be there when you need them? Remember that the person or persons whom you appoint cannot be compelled to act for you, so you should make sure that whoever it is that you appoint, will want to act for you. This is why it is important to appoint a back-up health care agent in case your first health care agent is unable or unwilling to act for you. Subject to the laws of your State, your health care agent will have various powers, including the ability to have access to your medical records, to deal with physicians, to deal with the possibility of your admission to a nursing home, etc. Having a Durable Power of Attorney for Health Care in place can help to reduce family friction and fighting because in that document you will be setting out in advance who you want to deal with these matters and what you want them to do.

10. In a situation where a couple is residing together, It is important that each of them have his or her own Durable Power of Attorney for Health Care.

11. You may have heard about a Living Will. It is often referred to as an advance directive. It is not the same as a Will. A Living Will addresses a situation where the following factors usually exist:

- A person may suffer from an illness or an injury which causes extreme physical or mental disability;
- The doctor believes that there is no reasonable expectation of that person's recovery.

In contemplation of such circumstances, such a person may express the wish that he or she not be kept alive by medication, artificial means or heroic measures. Furthermore, such a person may express the wish that his or her medication be mercifully administered and that surgical procedures be taken for the purpose of relieving him or her from suffering, even if such medication or such surgical procedures may shorten his or her remaining life.

12. In some jurisdictions the Living Will is one component of the Durable Power of Attorney for Health Care, but in other jurisdictions it may stand alone as a separate document. In all cases, however, you should speak to your doctor before preparing a Living Will. Your doctor should keep a copy of your Living Will with your medical records.

13. A Living Will will usually alleviate what your family will go through in instructing the doctor, in the event that your situation is so severe that there is no reasonable expectation that you will recover. If you fail to express your wishes this way, your family may have to guess at what your feelings are at a time when you cannot properly express your feelings. We should point out that before you do prepare your Living Will, it will be helpful to discuss these matters with your loved ones. If you do not have close relatives, your Living Will will at least provide guidance to the doctor.

14. If you are doing a Living Will on your own without professional assistance, you should make sure that it complies with the formalities required by your State and that it is based on the regulations of your own State and witnessed according to its formalities. It is recommended that you consult your lawyer before attempting to complete this document on your own.

15. A Living Will can be revoked at any time as long as you have capacity. If you rip it up it is gone. It is also important to periodically review your Living Will to make sure that it meets with your current wishes. A document you prepared five years ago may not meet with your needs today.

16. It is important to speak to your family, to get them involved and to let them know your wishes. Secrecy is not going to help you. It is often hard to talk about issues like terminal illness and death. As difficult as that may be, it is yet worse to keep silent about these issues. Silence can lead to turmoil and family disputes. Take a situation where you are very ill and one child tells the doctor "Dad wanted to be kept alive with machines at all costs", and another child tells the doctor "Dad did not want to be kept alive if there is no hope of recovery". You can only imagine the fights and conflicts that could ensue between the children. This is why it is so important to express your wishes in a Living Will.

17. A Living Will which cannot be found is of no use. You should therefore make sure that people know where to find your Living Will. One suggestion is to magnetize a card and leave it on your fridge to indicate to any medical personnel who may enter your home in the event of an emergency, that you have a health care agent and a Living Will. You might consider keeping a card in your purse or wallet in case of an accident, so that medical personnel who may find the card will be aware that you have a Living Will.

YOUR WILL

We have now seen the type of protection available to you in circumstances where you are alive, but by reason of illness or accident, unable to look after either your medical or your financial affairs. Both the Durable Power of Attorney for Property and the Durable Power of Attorney for Health Care are only effective during your life and have no validity after you have passed away. Accordingly it is now appropriate to ask the question "what happens after you die?" What measures are you putting into place to ensure that the assets that you worked so hard for during your life are distributed, without conflict, to those whom you choose to benefit from your estate? This is exactly where your Will fits in. Although no one likes to think of his or her own demise, we can probably all agree on one thing: there is no reason to procrastinate on preparing and signing a valid Will. It is a pivotal foundation to your estate planning. If you put this off, you may lose a week, then a month, then a year, and ultimately you may be at serious risk that the matter will never be a priority to you. The whole issue will continually occupy its place on the back burner. Those are the ingredients which will ultimately create some of the problems which we will be examining next. For all of us who have love and consideration for those we leave behind, having a proper Will in place should be a very, very high priority.

WHAT IF YOU DO NOT MAKE A WILL?

1. If you do not have a Will, the law of your State will set out who benefits after your death. If you pass away leaving a spouse and children, most States do not give your spouse your entire estate. Your spouse will have to share your estate with your children, according to a formula set out by State law. This can lead to conflict between your surviving spouse and your children.

State law does not give your best friend or your favorite charity a sum of money or any other benefit from your estate. Without a spouse, child or next of kin, everything you own will end up in the hands of the State, if you do not leave a Will.

If there is no Will, there is no executor appointed. Accordingly, there is no one in place to look after your estate after you die. This will compel someone to apply to court to obtain authority to carry out the functions which should have been conferred under a Will. Without a Will, you have not appointed a guardian to look after your minor children. For these and many other reasons you are creating a potential nightmare for your family if you do not prepare a Will. Remember, a Will is the final statement of your wishes to be effective after your death.

2. Some people trivialize Wills to the extent of trying to write their own Wills without obtaining professional assistance. This is a journey fraught with danger because the result may be an invalid Will. Your Will should be tailor made to your own particular life situation and should comply with the formalities dictated by the laws of your State. Your Will should be prepared by a professional skilled in the area. Many people who do not appreciate the complexities involved in this area of the law are reluctant to retain a lawyer to prepare their Wills because they feel that retaining a lawyer will create disproportionate expense for them. We would suggest that such a concern may be overstated, and in any event, what you pay for a Will is one of the best investments you will ever make.

WILLS

A Brief Introduction

1. Before you can make a Will, you must have legal capacity. For instance, one of the requirements of capacity is that you understand the nature and extent of your assets. For those who have lost their capacity through an accident or an illness, the unfortunate result is that they will not be able to make a valid Will. In addition to the question of capacity, the matter of doing the Will freely and voluntarily is an important consideration. If, after your death, someone can prove that you were forced into making your Will or changing it, that evidence will result in a successful challenge and the Will will be held invalid. That is why you sometimes hear that a Will has to be made freely and willingly and not under duress or undue influence. The third consideration is that of age. For example, in the State of Florida, a person who makes a Will must be of sound mind and at least 18 years of age. Not every State legislates 18 years as the age of majority. These comments with respect to the age of majority are correct as at the date of publication of this book. In addition to the capacity questions, you have to bear in mind that there are formal requirements which cannot be compromised. In almost every State, a

Will must be signed in front of at least two witnesses who must sign in the presence of each other and in the presence of the person making the Will.

2.   In your Will it is vital to set out the name of the person or persons you want to take control of your estate after your death. If you provide for more than one person, they are known as executors. If you provide for only one person, this person is referred to as an executor, or executrix in the female form. The executor you name in your Will will have the responsibility of looking after your estate after your death. For example, among other matters, the executor will pay your proper debts, will convert assets to cash where necessary in order to pay off debts and taxes and your executor will look after income tax filings and distribute your assets to your beneficiaries according to you Will. As noted previously, if you do not have a Will, no one will be appointed executor and someone will have to apply to the court to act in the capacity of what is commonly known as the administrator of your estate. We will be discussing more about your executor a little bit later.

3.   If you are parents of young children you should have a Will so that you can appoint a guardian to look after your children in the event you and your spouse were to be killed in an accident in circumstances where your children were not yet of the age of majority. If you do not have a Will which appoints a guardian of your minor children, someone will have to make a court application to appoint a guardian for such children. There is no guarantee that the person who applies to the court to become guardian will be granted guardianship by that court. Furthermore, there is also no guarantee that the person appointed by the court will be the same person you would have appointed in your Will, had you made one. Certainly, this can cause family conflict as, by way of example, in the case of opposing applications for guardianship launched by your wife's brother and your sister. With a proper guardianship appointment in your Will, you are likely to avoid this type of conflict.

4.   You should be aware that State law requires formalities to be followed in order for your Will to be valid. There are different witnessing requirements in different States. If your Will is not properly witnessed according to your State law, there could be a nightmare for your estate because the law will not recognize your Will as an enforceable document. As an aside, it should be recognized that some States allow Wills known as Holograph Wills. This type of Will differs from the formal Will we are discussing, because unlike a formal Will, it can be prepared in your own handwriting and does not require any witnesses. A Holograph Will would most likely be used when a person is in hospital and unable to get out to a lawyer to make a Will, but it is not in any way a recommended form of Will even if it is allowed by your State law. It is our recommendation that no matter which State you live in, you have a Will prepared based upon the formal requirements of your State. When we speak of formal requirements, we are including all requirements pertaining to the witnessing of your Will. We will not make any further reference to Holograph Wills in this book. With regard to witnesses, it is important to note that in most States a witness cannot be a beneficiary of your Will. This last point constitutes one of many pitfalls which may arise if you do a Will on your own without professional advice.

5. Once you have had your Will drafted by your lawyer, make sure you understand what it says. Remember, your Will is your document. It should reflect your wishes. As well, you may wish to sit down with your family and discuss the provisions in your Will. If you have any questions ask the lawyer preparing your Will to explain any clauses which you do not understand.

THE STRUCTURE
OF A WILL

You have been introduced to the subject matter of Wills. Perhaps this is the first time that the Will has in some degree been brought to life for you. You have also had some exposure to the problems that might arise if you pass away without a Will. In preparing this segment of the book, we realize how the fear and mystique of the subject matter has clouded the way people tend to think. In order to remove the fear and to remove the mystique, we want to bring you further into the subject in two stages, each of which will be easy for you to understand. In the first of these two stages, we explain the structure of a lawyer- prepared Will . Once you understand the structure, you will then be prepared for the second stage of our discussion, in which we will delve deeper into various components of a Will, with a view to showing you how they have to be carefully thought out in order to avoid or at least minimize family conflict after you pass away.

That brings us to the first of our two discussions. We will now summarize the basic structure of a Will. Generally speaking, a professionally drafted Will is composed of several parts:

1.   The Will must identify the person making it. If people commonly address you by a name other than the name on your birth certificate, you should tell your lawyer to insert both names in your Will in order to properly identify you and avoid problems for your beneficiaries. An example to illustrate this point would be: Charles Brooks, also known as Chuck Brooks.

2.   Generally speaking, your Will should cancel any prior Wills or other testamentary dispositions, such as a Codicil, which you may have made. The Codicil is an amendment to your original Will. However, there are exceptions to this general rule: There are unique estate situations where two Wills operating simultaneously are required in order to fulfill certain specialized requirements. An example would be where a person has substantial assets in different countries and may require a Will in each of those jurisdictions. This is a matter which should be discussed with your lawyer if you have concerns about this situation.

3.   The Will should appoint a primary executor or, if you wish to have more than one executor look after your estate, primary executors. It is important to appoint a back up in the event your executor or executors are unable or unwilling to look after your estate or in the event that they die before you. As a result, you should be naming one or more alternate executors.

4.   The Will should instruct your executor, or, if applicable, your executors, to pay or settle legitimate debts, claims and taxes owed by you before any assets are distributed to your beneficiaries under your Will.

5. The Will can distribute certain personal items, gifts of money or other assets, all of which are often referred to as legacies, to certain people whom you name to receive such legacies.

6. The Will should dispose of what is known as the residue of your estate. The residue consists of what is left after all of the debts and taxes have been paid and all of the specific legacies have been distributed. Every Will must have a residue clause.

7. The Will should provide for guardianship of your minor children, where applicable.

8. The Will should grant powers to your executors to enable them to look after your estate in an efficient manner.

9. You should sign your Will in front of at least two witnesses and ensure that you are complying with all of the legal formalities specified by your State. These formalities pertain to the ages of your witnesses, their capacity, and may include initialing at the bottom of every page of the Will by you and your witnesses.

Of course, there are certain optional provisions which are occasionally referred to in a Will, such as funeral and burial instructions and provisions relating to pets.

It is recommended that each person have his or her own Will. Whether you are in a relationship of husband and wife, a common law relationship or a same sex relationship, each of you should have your own Will. Some couples try to save costs by signing one Will. This is often referred to as a joint Will. If this is what you are contemplating, please consult with your lawyer to discuss the ramifications of a joint Will. You could potentially create a nightmare for your beneficiaries. Remember the expression "penny wise, pound foolish".

With these comments, we conclude our first discussion. We will now focus upon our second discussion, where we will delve more deeply into the various components of a Will, with a view to assisting you to maintain harmony within your family after you pass away.

ANALYSIS OF VARIOUS COMPONENTS OF A WILL

NAMING OF EXECUTORS

One of the most important estate planning decisions you can make is the choosing of the executor who will look after your estate when you

pass away. Essentially, your executor is the person appointed to make sure that your Will is properly carried out. For instance, among other things, your executor is responsible for arranging for the burial, making any claims on behalf of the estate, paying legitimate debts and taxes of your estate and satisfying the gifts made in your Will. You should choose one or more persons well suited to the duties required, and in making this choice, you should consider whether it is advantageous to select one executor, or several co-executors, as the case may be. You may also consider appointing a corporate entity as an executor. The corporate executor offers impartiality and permanence. In other words, you know that the corporate executor will be there. On the other hand, appointing a loved one or close family friend offers the advantage of intimate knowledge of your business and family needs. You might consider appointing your bank as your corporate executor, but if you do so you should consult your bank representative because many banks may be reluctant to accept an appointment as executor where the monetary value of the estate is below their minimum acceptable level. As you are speaking to your bank representative, you should also ask how much the institution will charge to manage your estate because that is a major consideration. Sometimes it is advisable to appoint an individual together with a corporate executor, as co-executors, assuming that such an appointment is acceptable to both parties. The following are some points you should consider when contemplating the choice of your executor:

(a) If you are leaving the entire estate outright to your spouse, you may consider the possibility of appointing your spouse as the sole executor if you feel that your spouse is capable of adminis-tering your estate.

(b) One common misconception pertains to the number of executors you are obliged to appoint. If you wish, you do have the right to appoint just one person as your executor.

(c) It may not be advisable to appoint as executor, the same person you are considering to be the guardian of your minor children. More particularly, imagine that the guardian has to take your two children in and build an extension to his house, severe-ly impairing his own cashflow. Is there justification for a guardian/executor to utilize the funds that you have put aside for your children, to fund the extension of the guardian's house? This conflict of interest can be avoided by ensuring that the per-son named as guardian is different from the person named as executor.

(d) You should consider whether the person you are appointing as executor has the time to take on the task. An executor may be trustworthy, but he or she may be unwilling to accept the appointment. Executors have the right to decline the appointment at the outset when they find out that they have been named. It is always advisable to obtain your executor's consent before naming him or her as executor. An executor's job is not an easy one. If you are considering appointing an executor who lives out of your State, you should discuss this with the lawyer preparing your Will. Make sure you tell your lawyer that your executor lives out of State. The law may impose certain requirements on an executor who resides out of your State.

(e) Your executor will have to make some management and business decisions. He or she will also have to deal with your grieving family. You should be aware that even though your executor may not have detailed business and management knowledge, he or she can hire professionals such as lawyers and accountants to deal with any complicated issues. If you do not think your children will get along with each other after your death, you may decide not to appoint any of your children as executors. Instead, you might wish to choose a neutral person or a financial institution.

(f) If you are appointing two co-executors, you should be aware that there can be a problem if they cannot agree on certain decisions. This could be expensive because it could lead to costly court applications. On the other hand, if you are appointing three or more co-executors, such as three of your adult children, you may consider inserting a majority clause in your Will to allow two of the three to make a binding decision. An example of such a decision would be the sale, or on the other hand the retention, of your house, after you die. This is a matter you should discuss with the professional who is drafting your Will.

(g) It is always a good idea to appoint one or more backup executors in case your first executor has predeceased you, or if he or she is unable or unwilling to act. A good example of such an appointment would be a person naming his or her spouse as primary executor and one or more of the adult children as back-up executors. What if the person or persons you named as primary executor, or primary executors, as the case may be, are not available to act on your behalf? Without a backup executor, your estate will be exposed to the risk of a court application in order to empower someone to deal with your estate.

(h) An executor is entitled to be paid for his or her work. Depending upon which State has jurisdiction, the compensation can take the form of a reasonable fee, perhaps a percentage of the estate. If you are appointing one of several children to be your executor, it would be wise to provide for a clause in your Will giving reasonable compensation to your executor, perhaps utilizing a formula such as a percentage or a set fee. By expressing yourself this way, you are easing the burden on that executor because the other children will know that you wished your executor to be paid for what he or she is doing on behalf of the estate. If you do not express this wish, the children who are not executors may put pressure on the child who is an executor not to take compensation. This can lead to bitterness and animosity. From the point of the view of the child who was appointed executor, what does he

47

or she do? Such an executor would be working very hard for the benefit of all of the children, but made to feel guilty about receiving compensation or reward for his or her hard work. A properly drafted clause in your Will can resolve this whole problem.

As we have discussed, your executor must pay your legitimate debts and taxes before any of the assets of your estate are distributed. Once the issues involving debts and taxes have been dealt with, your executor will be able to turn his or her attention to the distribution of your estate assets. That distribution of course must follow what your Will says. Some Wills provide for specific personal effects or gifts of money to be given to various beneficiaries. This is one area where a failure to devote the proper attention and the failure to obtain the proper professional advice can lead to unforeseen and unwelcome consequences, which are likely to result in family friction. When we speak of personal effects and gifts of money, we are speaking of issues that could be termed high risk because they are each capable of creating hostility among those you leave behind. For these reasons, we will now devote a specific discussion to each of these separate topics under their own headings.

PERSONAL EFFECTS

(a) If it is your intention to leave particular items in your Will to relatives and friends who have meant a lot to you, your thoughts are most likely to turn to particular items such as jewellery, antiques, paintings, furniture and collectible items. If you are going to leave specific personal effects of this nature in your Will, here is something to think about. What if the gift you are leaving is not there when you pass away? For example, you may wish to leave your sister your china figurine. If that figurine is broken or missing when you die, what gift, if any, will she get? This is why you may wish to instruct your lawyer to draft the Will so that a replacement gift will be provided to the person who would have received the original gift which was lost or destroyed. In the above example, a replacement gift  could be left for your sister, such as a crystal vase. Following this line of thought, what if the gift is there but your sister predeceases you? If you wish some other person to take the gift, you will have to speak to your lawyer about specifically providing for another person to receive it. For example, if your sister is not alive when you die, you might want her daughter to receive the gift in her place.

(b) In dealing with personal effects to be left under your Will, an interesting issue arises where you are in a second marriage. Here, it is quite common for one spouse to leave personal effects which he or she may have acquired in the first marriage to the children of that marriage. A prime example would be the leaving of family heirlooms to children of your first marriage. If this is what you wish to do, you should advise your lawyer of your specific intention to leave these personal effects to the children of your first marriage. At the front of your mind, what you are attempting to avoid is a situation where the spouse of your second marriage takes the heirlooms on the authority of a generally worded Will which leaves everything to him or to her. In such a situation, you can now begin to see the conflict which can arise if the broken hearted children of your first marriage have to plead with the spouse of your second marriage in order to get back their treasured memories. Of course, when we talk about treasured memories, we not only refer to what was acquired early in their childhood, but also to what was handed down through the generations.

(c) If you have a list of personal effects which you wish to distribute under your Will, you can speak to your lawyer about preparing a binding memorandum for the purpose of distributing such personal items among your beneficiaries. This binding memorandum would be incorporated by reference in your Will. You should be aware that such a memorandum cannot be changed unless you prepare a proper legal amendment to your Will known as a Codicil, or unless you prepare a brand new Will. If one or more of the items referred to in the memorandum becomes lost, destroyed or sold, the memorandum will of course be out of date. This situation could compel you to prepare a Codicil or a brand new Will. You should also be aware that there are certain legal requirements to comply with when you prepare a memorandum of this nature and you will have to speak to your lawyer about signing, dating and witnessing the document to ensure that it is binding.

(d) If you find that a binding memorandum is too restrictive for your requirements, there is another alternative available to you. It is sometimes referred to as a non binding personal effects memorandum. It is not binding on your executor but it does express your wishes as to who will get what after you die. This type of memorandum is not part of your Will but it is usually kept with your personal papers. Because of its non binding nature, it would apply more to items of sentimental value than to items of monetary value. One word of advice: It would not be wise to utilize a non- binding memorandum to give items of significant value.

Let's end this discussion with a few practical points relating to personal effects:

1. In your Will or memorandum, avoid using general phrases such as "my antiques" because such phrases are hard to define and may create confusion and even arguments among your beneficiaries. For example, it is quite clear that an antique would be descriptive of an item which was from the era of the 19th century. However, it is not so clear that an item manufactured during the 1950's is an antique. The search for definition may well lead your beneficiaries to the courthouse.

2. If you are leaving a gift to someone who lives far away, who will pay for the costs of packing, storage and freight? Your Will should make clear who is to be responsible for these charges. Your failure to specify the party who has the obligation to pay for such charges is likely to cause the recipient of the gift to argue with your estate over who will bear the costs, if such costs are substantial.

3. Your Will or memorandum must adequately identify the gift you are leaving. For example, if you have three diamond rings, each of which has separate characteristics, and each of which has a different value, you are sowing the seeds of a fight if, in your Will or memorandum, you say "I give my diamond ring to my daughter, Mary Smith". An example of proper identification would be something to the following effect: "To give to my daughter, Mary Smith, my 18 carat diamond gold ring with the inscription of my initials on the inside of the ring".

4. It is often helpful to prepare a videotape to assist you in describing the gifts which you are leaving in your Will or memorandum.

5. From a common sense point of view, if there are certain maintenance instructions which are necessary to preserve or maintain a gift which you are leaving to someone in your Will, you should take some steps to pass along those instructions to your executor or beneficiary, as the case may be.

In addition to, or as an alternative to a gift of a specific item, you may consider leaving one or more gifts of money to one or more beneficiaries in your Will. Let us examine a couple of issues relating to this matter.

GIFTS OF MONEY

With regard to leaving gifts of money under your Will, consider the following important matters:

(a) The gift which you intend to leave will be effective only if there is enough money in your estate to satisfy that gift. Accordingly, you must consider whether, at the time of your death, there will be enough money in your estate to fund the various cash gifts that you are thinking of leaving to your beneficiaries. A shortfall in such funding can cause confusion and acrimony among your beneficiaries because the gifts will not be capable of payment as you contemplated in your Will. Furthermore, even if at the time of your death there will be enough cash to fund all of these gifts, you must remember that all of your debts and taxes have to be paid in full before any cash gifts can be distributed to your beneficiaries.

(b) There is one fundamental piece of advice which applies to every gift which you are providing for in your Will, including the gifts of money which we are referring to in this section. It is always prudent to name one or more substitute beneficiaries to take the gift in the event that your primary beneficiary passes away before you do.

(c) Conflicts among your beneficiaries could arise from what is sometimes known as an unintended double legacy. That term describes a situation where a beneficiary under your Will who is to receive one gift of money in the event of a common disaster, such as a motor vehicle accident, ends up receiving two gifts of money as a result of the death of both parties in that common disaster. In considering this matter, let us first start off with the question of intention. In the case of a husband and wife each leaving $10,000.00 to their grandson Robert, is it their intention that Robert receive two gifts of $10,000.00 in the event that the husband and wife are involved in a common disaster and pass away? Or, on the other hand, is it their intention that Robert inherit the $10,000.00 gift only once, on the death of the last to die of the husband and wife? This is a situation which is often overlooked and which is capable of creating havoc within your family. If your lawyer is not advised of your intention, and the matter becomes overlooked, an unintended windfall of this nature can be a great source of dissension among those who survive

53

you because the unintended gift will reduce what is left to distribute among the other beneficiaries.

CHARITABLE GIFTS

You may wish to give something to a charity under your Will and if you do, you should be considering the following points:

(a) In your Will, you may wish to benefit a charity by leaving a particular sum of money or perhaps a share of your estate. It is important that you name the charity correctly and that your lawyer inserts that correct name in your Will. You can obtain the exact legal name of your favorite charity by contacting them. You should also speak to your accountant about any possible tax benefits available by leaving charitable gifts in your Will.

(b) If you die without a Will your favorite charity will not benefit from your estate. The law sets out who will inherit and a charity is not considered a beneficiary under the law.

(c) Make sure you speak to your lawyer about what happens if the charity named in your Will does not exist at the time of your death. Do you wish a similar charity to benefit or do you want the gift that was left to such charity to fall into your estate and to be shared by your other beneficiaries?

RESIDUE

(a) We discussed the various types of gifts you can make in your Will. We discussed giving specific gifts of personal items, furniture, etc. We discussed the gift of a sum of money leaving, for example, $10,000.00 to your friend. Now we will discuss the residue of the estate. In order to understand what residue is, think of everything you own at the time of your death. From that total amount, subtract what is needed in order to pay your debts, administrative expenses and taxes, and from that take out all of the gifts of money and other assets that we have just talked about. Everything else left over is known as the residue of your estate.

(b) It is important to name people or charities to benefit from the residue: otherwise the law will set out who inherits it. In a first marriage situation, it is quite common for each spouse to leave the entire residue to the other and upon the decease of both spouses, the residue is usually split among the children in equal shares. In other words, if your spouse is not alive at your death or you die together, your children will split the residue equally. Be very careful, however, about leaving the entire residue of your estate to your spouse in a second marriage situation. Doing so, could lead to a fight between your spouse and the children of your first marriage. If your spouse survives you, there is nothing to stop him or her from making a brand new Will cutting out the children of your first marriage and conferring all of the benefits of your own hard work upon his or her own family or children. This consideration will apply, of course, if it is your intention to protect the children of your first marriage.

GUARDIANSHIP

If you have minor children, your Will should appoint one or more guardians to look after them in the event you and your spouse both pass away before your children reach the age of majority. In the event that you

 do not have a Will, or, if you have a Will which does not deal with the matter of guardianship, someone will have to apply to court to be appointed guardian of your minor children. That person could be a family member or a friend. You might wonder at this point how the failure to name a guardian can lead to family conflict. Imagine the situation which would arise if you and your spouse unexpectedly passed away together in an accident leaving minor children. Imagine further that you did not leave a Will, or alternatively, you left a Will but it did not provide for guardianship. In such circumstances it is perfectly possible that your spouse's sister and your brother might have been very close to your children. It is reasonable that each of them might apply to become guardian of your minor children. If they cannot resolve the issue between them, it is extremely unlikely that a court would appoint both of them. These are the circumstances in which they would be battling each other in court for the custody of your children.

Guardianship should not be looked at in the abstract. When you name a guardian, you have to be aware that you may be imposing serious financial obligations on your guardian or guardians, as the case may be. Accordingly, you must direct your mind to the proper funding of the guardianship and you might also consider compensating your guardians in the appropriate circumstances.

In addition to the above considerations, there are a number of other important points pertaining to guardianship which you might wish to consider. In examining these points, we will be using the singular version, but bear in mind that you do have the right at all times to name a couple as guardians:

(a) Some people name the same person as both executor and guardian. Although we have previously raised this point in our discussion of the topic of executorship, the issue is so important that it deserves its own emphasis, once again. To repeat then, this combination could lead to a potential conflict of interest and it is not the most prudent way to proceed. By separating your guardian from your executor, you are establishing checks and balances within the administration of your estate. How would you feel if one person occupied both positions, and used the funds designated for the raising of your children to add an extension to his or her own home in order to accommodate your children? If, in this example, an extension of the home were really necessary, at least you would have a separate party considering the necessity of such construction. This would certainly enhance the best interests of your children. This illustrates why it is usually advisable to have one person look after your funds in the capacity of executor and another person looking after the interests of your children in the capacity of guardian.

(b) Be careful about appointing a married couple as guardians. You should feel very confident about their ability to get along together before concluding an appointment of this nature. If they get separated or divorced, who will have custody of your children? For example, if you appoint your brother and his wife as guardians, and after your death they separate, will there be a custody battle for your children ?. To solve this, it might be prudent to appoint your brother alone.

(c) Your parents are not always the best choice as guardians because they may not outlive you and if they do they may be elderly or unable to act.

(d) While it is understood that your Will expresses your intention to appoint a guardian, you might consider leaving a document apart from your Will which sets out your thoughts and your wishes as they relate to the upbringing of your children. Such wishes may pertain to the education and lifestyle of your children, among other matters. These thoughts can be expressed in a letter, and may serve to resolve issues between your guardians and your minor children.

(e) A practical point: Make sure to leave the full legal name and address and telephone number of each person you are naming as guardian. This point may sound trivial, but your executor may be hard pressed to find your guardian without a designated address and telephone number. This is the type of matter that should be kept up to date as the years go on.

(f) It is a good idea to name a backup guardian in case your primary guardian becomes unable or unwilling to carry out the function, or in the event that he or she passes away before you do.

(g) Do not presume that your guardian will automatically accept the appointment. It is important to tell your proposed guardian of your intention to appoint him or her in your Will. In considering this appointment, remember that the guardianship may add stresses to the guardian's life. Appreciate as well the pressures that may be imposed upon your guardian's family situation, especially, if your guardian has his or her own children.

(h) It is important to periodically review your Will to ensure that the guardian arrangements that you have set out in your Will are up to date.

EXECUTOR POWERS

In order to achieve an efficient administration of your estate, it is imperative that you provide your executor or executors with adequate powers. Failure to provide such executor powers in your Will, as is the case in many homemade Wills, can impose significant burdens on your executors and on your estate. The powers that you failed to grant to your executors in your Will may have to be obtained by your executors through a court application. This imposes delay, expense and some element of uncertainty in the administration of your estate. Such a situation will not have a calming effect upon your beneficiaries who are awaiting finalization and closure in the matter of your estate.

Most professionally drafted Wills contain, among other powers, a power to sell estate assets, a power to retain estate assets in the form in which they exist at the time of the decease, and a power to borrow against estate assets in order to raise funds for necessary purposes. Without such a power to borrow, if your executors require money in order to pay estate debts and taxes, they may have to resort to selling estate assets instead of borrowing against those assets. For all of these reasons, among others, you should be asking your lawyer to tell you what executor powers he or she recommends in your Will.

SIGNING AND WITNESSING YOUR WILL

The law in most jurisdictions imposes rather strict formalities upon those in the process of signing a Will. You should rely upon your lawyer to arrange the appropriate witnessing requirements. If you choose to do your Will on your own, without the assistance of a lawyer, it is important to be aware that some jurisdictions require more than two witnesses. Your witnesses have to be present with you and must be in the presence of each other when you sign the Will. It is most advisable to insert your initials at the bottom of each page of the Will and beside the date. Your witnesses should also provide their initials in the same places as you do. Speak to your lawyer about preparing a self-proving Affidavit which can help to lessen the formal requirements involved in the probate process.

If it is your wish to minimize stress and anxiety for your family, ensure that your Will can be found after you pass away. Many lawyers can tell you stories about the strange locations of the Wills of their clients. Wills have been found in the pocket of an arm chair between two magazines. They have been found in freezers, under kitchen sinks, in kitchen cupboards, dining room drawers, night table drawers and even in cardboard boxes with outdated personal papers. The search for this crucial document can prove to be disproportionately time-consuming and upsetting. There is of course the risk that the Will may never be found. For all of these reasons, many people choose to leave the formally signed and witnessed Will in the safe custody of their lawyers. Many others keep their Wills in their safety deposit boxes at their banks. This procedure is perfectly acceptable, but you should realize that access to your safety deposit box will be very limited once you pass away. The bank is very likely to impose hurdles and restrictions upon those who wish to view the contents of a safety deposit box. Finally, there are those who insist upon keeping the Will at home, which is reasonably acceptable provided that the Will is kept in a fireproof container and that the executor knows where to find the Will.

FREQUENTLY ASKED ESTATE PLANNING QUESTIONS

Up to this point, we have seen how your Durable Powers of Attorney and your Will fit into the general estate planning process. As well, we have begun to see why having these documents is so important if your goal is to avoid family fighting. In our discussion, we have seen the significance of focusing on the elements of which these documents are composed, in order to accomplish the various objectives of protecting yourself during your lifetime, protecting your loved ones in the event of your incapacity or decease, and maintaining family harmony. However, the matter does not end there. Now we will take the matter another step further and address questions which are likely to arise in the process of thinking all of these matters through. We recognize of course that the entire field is so broad that an unlimited number of questions can in theory arise. To address all of them would evidently be well beyond the scope of this book. What we will concentrate on are the following questions:

- When you make your Will do you have to leave everything to your beneficiaries outright or can you distribute to some beneficiaries outright and have your trustees hold back property or money gifts for other beneficiaries until those beneficiaries reach a certain age?

- Can you cut your spouse out of your Will?
- Can you cut one or more children out of your Will?
- How does property held between yourself and another person affect your Will?
- If you have a Will, when should you review it?
- If you have a Will, how do you change it?
- Can you make a homemade Will?

OUTRIGHT GIFTS VS. HOLDING MONEY IN TRUST

In approaching this subject, it should be recognized that we are talking about a situation that will only arise after you pass away. You should be aware that there are separate planning instruments which can be utilized during your lifetime. Sometimes they are known as living trusts. These planning instruments are often used for various purposes, such as tax planning and avoiding or minimizing probate. They are beyond the ambit of this book, and if you are interested in more information on living trusts, you should speak to a lawyer who is familiar with this area of the law. That having been said, we now focus upon the situation which arises within your Will, which of course addresses what happens after you pass away.

In putting your mind to the subject matter of any gift that is going to be given under your Will, one of the most important considerations is whether that gift should be given outright as soon as you die or whether the gift should be held in trust until, for example, your beneficiary reaches a certain age beyond the age of majority. If you give the gift outright in your Will, your beneficiary, who has attained the age of majority, can do whatever he or she wants with that gift when you pass away without having any control imposed on his or her decision making. Where you are setting up a trust in your Will, you are not giving the gift outright to your beneficiary on your death. The gift will be managed and invested by your executor until the event occurs which allows the beneficiary to take the gift in accordance with your Will. There are three points that should be raised at this stage:

- We are usually talking about gifts of money;
- We are assuming that the amount of money is not trivial because the administration of the trust would be disproportionately expensive if the gift involved were very small;
- There are some trusts which allow the executor to provide income to the beneficiary during the beneficiary's life, but the nature of these trusts is such that the beneficiary will never receive the capital of the gift during his or her lifetime because the capital will be given to a different beneficiary. Such trusts are commonly known as life interests.

Now that you have, in general terms, seen the basic distinction between an outright gift in a Will and a gift held in trust, we will address some practical considerations that you must keep in mind.

(a) Many parents feel that an outright gift to a child is not practical because those parents do not want that child to inherit a large sum of money outright when he or she reaches the age of majority. The parents would rather have the money managed and invested until the child reaches a more mature age. This is accomplished by setting up a trust in your Will as indicated above. You can pick an age at which you feel your child will be mature enough to inherit outright. By setting up a trust in your

Will, you can ensure that your executor, a person you trust, is managing and investing your child's money until that child reaches the age which you specified. This treatment is very different from an outright gift to your child at the age of majority, because in such a case, your child will be able to get his or her hands on the money and spend it, according to his or her whim. Imagine your child, not yet twenty years old, taking a big block of cash and buying an expensive sports car. From your point of view you would much rather see that same money being kept available to fund a college education for your child. This demonstrates why it is often important to set up a trust in your Will.

(b) An important consideration in setting up a trust in your Will, also known as a testamentary trust, is to select the proper person to act as executor. The term executor, for the purposes of this book, should be regarded as interchangeable with the term trustee. You should be aware that you can have multiple executors. For illustrative purposes we will assume that you have named only one executor. You may wish to consider a neutral person or a financial institution as opposed to one of your children to act as the trustee for your other child's money. Knowing your family as you do, you should consider whether problems could arise if one child is governing the funds set aside for his or her sibling.

(c) If you are setting up a trust for your child until he or she reaches an age such as twenty-five, you can have your Will drafted so that your trustee has access to the funds required for your child's maintenance, education, advancement, medical needs or any other matters which your trustee feels necessary for the general benefit of your child. This is commonly known as a power of invasion or encroachment. These two terms are used interchangeably. Your executor will have the ability to take money for your child's legitimate needs as described above. Even though your child's share of the principal will be frozen until your child reaches the age which you specify in your Will, your trustee can nevertheless access the principal for those needs which the trustee feels require the expense of capital. It is obvious that your trustee is exercising a large amount of discretion over what money is going to be available to your child or for the benefit of your child. The trustee is carrying out his or her obligations as stated in your Will, but there may be occasional conflict between your trustee and your child. In order to smooth out areas of conflict, it might be advisable for you to write a letter, separate and apart from your Will, expressing your true feelings about the type of discretion that your trustee should exercise after your death. For example, in this type of a letter you may express your wish that the trustee can use the child's money for educational purposes but cannot use the money for an expensive European vacation or an expensive sports car. A letter of this nature can be of great comfort to your trustee because he or she can show your child the letter that sets out your true wishes as to how the trust money is to be treated.

The type of trust being described in this paragraph, being a trust which includes a power of invasion or encroachment, is not the only type of trust that you can set up in your Will. You also have the ability to set up a trust where there is no power of invasion or encroachment whatsoever. This would prevent the trustee from encroaching upon the principal amount of the trust, even in situations where your child may be in desperate need.

This subject, as you can see, is sufficiently important that it merits a serious discussion with your professional advisor.

(d) You should be aware that you could set up your Will so that the ages at which your beneficiaries inherit money is staggered. For example, you may provide that one quarter of the money to be inherited is given to your beneficiaries when each of them obtains the age of twenty-one years. You may then consider that another quarter is similarly given to them when each of them attains the age of twenty-five years, and the balance might be given to them at the age of twenty-eight years.

(e) In considering these trust arrangements, there are a few matters which you should definitely canvass with your lawyer in the course of giving instructions to draft your Will:

- There may be restrictions imposed upon how long you have the right to defer the payment of the income;
- There may be restrictions imposed upon how long you can defer the payout of the capital;
- You should provide for a backup beneficiary in the event that the beneficiary who is supposed to receive the principal of the trust, fails to attain the specified age.

(f) The trust can be a useful vehicle in a second marriage situation. It allows you to benefit the children of your first marriage while at the same time providing adequate protection to your second spouse. One version of this form of a trust consists of giving a life interest to your second spouse in the whole of, or in a part of, your estate, thereby preserving your assets so that they can be given to the children of your first marriage when your second spouse passes away. This life interest allows your second spouse to be comfortable because he or she has the use of your assets, but this life interest will not allow your second spouse to leave any of the assets held in this trust through his or her Will. The reason why your second spouse will not be able to give away your assets in his or her Will is simply because that life interest provides for possession or use, but does not provide for ownership. Ultimately, when your second spouse passes away, the life interest we have just described comes to an end. It is at that stage that the children of your first marriage or the other beneficiaries whom you wanted to inherit from you, will take the assets which were preserved in this manner.

Depending upon your wishes and the needs of your second spouse, you could structure the life interest so that your trustee will have the power to encroach upon the assets of which the life interest is composed in favor of your second spouse, for his or her medical or other legitimate needs. However, this is a very delicate question because encroachment which favors the lifestyle requirements of your second spouse will result in a reduction in the amount to be inherited by the children of your first marriage. In other words, increasing the money paid to your second spouse out of the capital of your estate by way of encroachment results mathematically in less being left for your other beneficiaries when your second spouse passes away. The balancing of these contending interests can prove to be very stressful for your trustee. For this reason, many Wills provide very limited rights of encroachment to the trustee and other Wills provide for no right of encroachment at all. In view of the balancing function that your trustee is likely to be called upon to perform, it is evident that you must exercise caution in making that appointment. You should decide in favor of neutrality in balancing the interests of your second spouse against the interests of the beneficiaries who will be inheriting after that second spouse passes away. We should, for illustrative purposes, examine this subject as if the trustee named were not neutral. On the one hand, imagine naming your second spouse as trustee in circumstances where your Will provides for him or for her to encroach upon the capital of your trust. It is almost inevitable that the second spouse in such circumstances would be tempted to leave less for distribution to the children of your first marriage, in our example. On the other hand, looking at the other side of the equation, if you named one of the children of your first marriage as trustee, that child would be tempted to adopt a very conservative approach toward the question of lifestyle of your second spouse. The more that the child of your first marriage encroaches in favor of your second spouse, the less he or she will receive when your second spouse passes away. In order to adhere to neutrality, you must be very selective and exercise considerable wisdom in your choice of trustee, and this will very often lead to your selecting a financial institution to fulfill this role.

A spousal trust is not a matter to be taken lightly. If it is not treated properly, it can, in some jurisdictions, create adverse tax consequences. Furthermore, if you have not signed a marriage contract which eliminates a spousal right of election, your efforts to protect the children of your first marriage in this manner may be frustrated. Depending upon where you live, your spouse may have the right to elect to receive a certain portion of the property of your estate after you pass away, even if the wording of your Will either cuts out your spouse or limits his or her rights to inherit from you. We will now focus in more detail on the subject of cutting your spouse out of your Will.

CAN YOU CUT YOUR SPOUSE OUT OF YOUR WILL?

In the paragraph above, reference is made to the right of a spouse to elect. A right to elect will exist in those States which have laws designed to protect a surviving spouse against being cut out of a Will or being left an inadequate amount in a Will by his or her deceased spouse. A spousal right of election gives a surviving spouse the right to decide whether he or she is going to accept what is left in the Will of the deceased spouse or whether he or she will claim his or her entitlement under the law. Many States have laws which offer this type of protection to a surviving spouse.

Some people think that by leaving one dollar to a spouse, they can circumvent these provisions. However the surviving spouse will still have the right to make the election described above, if the law of his or her jurisdiction provides for such an election. The nature of this spousal election allows your spouse to take these steps even if you leave your spouse assets in a large trust in your Will. Finally, depending upon where you live, the amount that your spouse receives as a beneficiary under your life insurance policy could reduce his or her entitlement to the amount payable under a spousal election.

We have seen from the above discussion that in jurisdictions which provide for spousal election rights, any attempt which you make to cut your spouse out of your Will will fail if your spouse chooses to exercise his or her election rights. In the absence of such election rights, you should be consulting your lawyer to determine whether there are other similar protections for a surviving spouse who is cut out of a

Will. Your lawyer may have to consider other matters before giving you a clear opinion as to your ability to either totally cut your spouse out of your Will or to leave him or her a token amount.

You should speak to a family law lawyer about a marriage contract. In this contract, you and your spouse could agree to follow the terms of each other's Wills and waive your election rights. Such a marriage contract will protect your estate from the claims of your surviving spouse.

CAN YOU CUT YOUR CHILD OUT OF YOUR WILL?

In many jurisdictions, the word "child" or "children" includes children born of your marriage, children you have adopted, children born out of wedlock and children from a prior marriage. It is important to address this question with your lawyer, to ensure that the definition applies to your situation. Assuming that your situation falls within the definition, you must then consider a presumption of law which applies in most jurisdictions in the United States. That presumption of law is best expressed by the term "pretermitted heir". In plain language, the presumption is that you intended to include the omitted child on the grounds that the omission was inadvertent. To illustrate this concept, suppose your children are named Peter, Bill, John and Mary and it is your intention to cut John out by not naming him in your Will. Your attempt will run afoul of the pretermitted heir rules, and John will be included, unless you find a method of circumventing the presumption. Without attempting to provide legal advice here, your lawyer might possibly suggest to you that if you really do wish to cut John out, your Will should at least make reference to John, make reference to your intention to cut him out, and your lawyer should insert proper wording in your Will so that you can rebut the presumption of the pretermitted heir.

Another consideration involves dependent children. Your State may have laws which might prevent you from cutting dependent children out of your Will. Again, you should speak to your lawyer about this. Where these laws apply, your dependent children may be able to launch a court application against your estate in order that they receive support from your estate. You should speak to your lawyer about the definition of dependent child or dependent children in your jurisdiction.

HOW DOES PROPERTY JOINTLY HELD BETWEEN YOURSELF AND ANOTHER PERSON AFFECT YOUR WILL?

Where you hold property such as real estate or a bank account jointly with another person, this form of holding is often referred to as joint ownership with right of survivorship. From a legal point of view, when one of such joint owners passes away, the property will automatically go to the other joint owner or owners, as the case may be. If the joint owner who passed away left a Will, what many people do not understand is that the person who left the Will ceases to be the owner of the jointly held property at the time of his or her death. As a result, his or her Will is going to be incapable of transferring the property which had been held in joint ownership. The surviving joint owner is the one who gets the property regardless of what the deceased joint owner's Will provided for. To illustrate this point, if you and your brother own a farm as joint owners with right of survivorship and you prepare a Will leaving the farm to your son, if you die before your brother does, it is your brother and not your son who will own the farm. Your Will can only leave what you own. It cannot leave what you do not own, and by the operation of the right of survivorship, your brother owns the farm so it cannot be left under your Will to anybody. As you might imagine, this can create serious conflict between your brother and your son. Your son sees what you expressed in your Will, and thinks he is entitled to the farm, yet he cannot receive it because of the circumstances as recited above.

It is important to deal with a professional advisor, especially on this point, because in certain jurisdictions, there may be exceptions to this rule. One example can be found in a certain jurisdiction where you may own your family home in joint ownership with a person other than your spouse. The law of that particular jurisdiction will sever the joint tenancy by operation of law so that the property will not automatically go to your brother, and the law will preserve your spouse's interest in the family home.

You should be aware that holding a property with another person can take many forms. Joint ownership, as described above, is only one type of property holding. Another type of property holding is sometimes referred to as tenants in common. This type of ownership is similar to partnership. If you and your brother own a farm as tenants in common, it means that upon your death, your interest in the farm will pass according to the provisions of your Will, and will not automatically go to your brother. Similarly, he is in the same situation.

We have seen in the above discussions how you can encounter various restrictions which impede you from dealing with your own assets in your Will. Thus far, we have seen this point illustrated in our discussion regarding your spouse, your child and joint owners. Before leaving this subject, we should draw to your attention a few business considerations which will similarly have a restrictive effect upon your planning:

- Partnership or shareholder agreements which relate to your business interests in a firm or a corporation may prevent you from leaving those interests to a beneficiary because your co partners or co shareholders may have either a right of first refusal or an option to purchase which places their interests in priority to the interests of the beneficiaries named in your Will;

- Similarly, a franchise agreement is likely to contain provisions which apply to the transfer of the franchise at the time of your death. Some of those provisions may require the person to whom you are leaving the franchised business to qualify as a franchisee. You cannot assume that in every case, the person you name as beneficiary in your Will is going to succeed in qualifying as a franchisee in the event that your beneficiary applies to the franchisor to take over the business;

- If you are a member of a profession such as doctor, lawyer or dentist, you will not be able to leave your professional practice to someone who is not a member of your profession. For example, your spouse cannot continue your practice as a lawyer unless he or she is already a lawyer.

WHEN SHOULD YOU REVIEW YOUR WILL?

Once you have signed your Will, you may put the document away safely, breathe a sigh of relief and move forward with your life. However, be aware that the story does not end when you put your Will away in a safe place. You must still review this most important document, both periodically and when a major event will change your life situation. Let's look at how changes in your life situation can affect your Will:

MARRIAGE OR RE-MARRIAGE

In many jurisdictions, a marriage completely revokes a previously made Will. For example, if you made a Will in 1989 and you married in 1991, in all likelihood the Will you made in 1989 will be revoked. Some jurisdictions do provide for exceptions to this situation. An example of such an exception would be a Will made in contemplation of a marriage. Such a Will contains a statement making reference to the upcoming marriage. In jurisdictions which allow for it, a Will in contemplation of marriage is perfectly valid and will survive marriage. You should speak to your lawyer to determine whether the law of your State allows for this exception.

When we consider that a marriage revokes a Will, subject to the above exception of course, it makes no difference whether the marriage is a first marriage or a subsequent marriage.

DIVORCE

In many States, a divorce will affect what was contained in your Will. Whether your Will survives a divorce depends upon the law of your State. Divorce will revoke your Will in its entirety in some States, whereas a Will may survive a divorce, except for the gifts left to your ex-spouse, in other States. Because of the complexity of this situation, it is extremely important that you obtain advice from your legal representative.

The above comments relate to a Will as opposed to a policy of insurance or assets which are held jointly with right of survivorship. Even though a Will itself may be revoked by a subsequent marriage or, as we have seen, in some cases, a divorce, the insurance policy which names the spouse as beneficiary can easily survive that marriage or divorce, notwithstanding the revocation of the Will. The same principle applies to property held jointly with right of sur-vivorship. For example, you may think that your Will has been taken care of by divorce, forgetting the windfall that your ex-spouse may get if he or she remains as beneficiary on your life insurance policy. If you are about to get married or divorced, it is imperative that you sit down with your lawyer to review not only your Will, but all of the insurance policies, jointly held property and other assets which you may have in order to avoid surprises.

SEPARATION

Contrast the situation that arises under a separation, with that of a divorce. When you are separated, you are, in law, still married. As a result, if you have named your spouse as beneficiary in your Will, in most jurisdictions he or she will benefit from your Will, notwithstand-ing your separation. Of course, protection is available from this situation through a separation agreement, which would provide for a release of your estate, among many other matters. If in the context of a separation, it is your intention not to benefit the spouse from whom you are sepa-rating, it is important that you review with your legal advisor, not only your Will, but also insurance policy designations, property owned in joint ownership with right of survivorship and your various other assets.

OTHER EVENTS

Let us touch on a few other events which should prompt you to review your Will:

- Children born since the date of your Will;
- Grandchildren born since the date of your Will;
- Incapacity or death of a beneficiary named in your Will;

- Incapacity, frailty or death of your executor;
- Loss of trust or confidence in your executor;
- Changes in the law of your State;
- Your move to a new State;
- Sale of, loss of, or damage to an item which you have gifted in your Will.

HOW DO YOU CHANGE YOUR WILL?

If it is your wish to make changes to your Will, you should never do so without consulting a lawyer. The law governing changes is very formal and very strict.

If you attempt to make changes to your Will but fail to follow the required formalities, the end result will be that the Will that you made originally will continue to be effective, and that the changes you attempted to make will be of no force or effect whatsoever. You would certainly be ill advised to make deletions, notations and markings on your original Will for these reasons. Suppose, for example, you name your good friends John and Mary as executors. Subsequently, you have a falling out with John. You decide to name your brother William as co-executor with Mary and to save costs, you simply scratch out John's name and insert your brother William's name in your original Will. You do this without consulting any professional, and you do not realize that what you have done deviates in its entirety from the prescribed methods of amending a Will. You file your Will away and no one sees the original again until after you pass away. It is only then, for the first time, that the gravity of this error emerges. John, the one person whom you wanted to be removed from the situation, has full authority from your Will as it was originally drafted, and now insists upon exercising that authority. William, the person in whom you have placed substantial trust, has no status because he was never legally appointed to be executor. You now have a situation where Mary is compelled to work with John instead of William. This illustrates how important it is to obtain the proper advice in dealing with any changes to be made to your Will. You may appreciate that the naming of an unintended executor in this case may be minor, compared to what could potentially happen if, instead of the name of the executor being scratched out, it was the name of a beneficiary which was scratched out. You can easily see how ineffective changes to your Will can result in fighting among your family members.

If you wish to avoid situations of this nature, obtain the proper legal advice before making any changes to your Will. If the changes which you have in mind are major, in all likelihood you will receive advice to the effect that you should make a brand new Will. For changes of a more minor nature, you will most likely receive advice to make the changes by means of what is known as a Codicil. A Codicil is the legal term used to describe a formal change to your Will. It is possible to have more than one Codicil to your Will. After you pass away, your Will is read together with the Codicils which you have made.

WHAT ABOUT HOMEMADE WILLS?

Throughout this book, we have emphasized the importance of getting proper legal advice. Despite everything we have said, we recognize that there are people out there who are determined to prepare their own Will without professional advice. They are travelling a very risky path. Their margins of error are narrow and their mistakes may impose years of conflict upon those who survive them.

If you are intent on writing your own Will, you should be aware that there are many pitfalls which await the amateur. Some of these pitfalls lead to invalidity, others lead to failed gifts, and others lead to family conflict. We have seen many problems with homemade Wills. Many of the homemade Wills which we have seen failed to:

1. appoint backup executors and guardians;

2. name backup beneficiaries;

3. identify charities properly;

4. use language specific enough to identify the gift being left;

5. recognize that events do not always happen in the order that people expect them to. For instance, children do not always outlive their parents;

6. contain sufficient administrative powers necessary to enable the named executor to efficiently administer the estate, thereby compelling the executor to seek these powers from a court;

7. follow the legally required formalities of signing and witnessing.

These are only some of the problems which we have seen arising from our review of homemade Wills.

THE IMPORTANCE OF ORGANIZING YOUR AFFAIRS

Helping to Minimize the Stress on Your Loved Ones

Your incapacity or death will most likely be very traumatic for your loved ones. Proper organization of your affairs will go a long way toward easing the burden upon them.

Imagine your loved ones rummaging through your home and your safety deposit box in circumstances of your incapacity or death. In our imaginary scenario, we have them gathering up all of the papers they can find. However, they do not know if what they have found is up to date, nor how importantly they rank amongst other documentation, and they have no way of knowing whether what they found represents only a part of the full story of your financial affairs. In any event, all they can really do is to stuff the papers into plastic bags and go for help. Help most often leads to the office of a professional, such as a lawyer or an accountant. From our own point of view, we look upon a situation such as this as both stressful and chaotic. As professionals, we look upon what we have just described as being very far removed from a properly organized financial situation.

Let us take this matter just a little bit further, based upon what we have observed in our own law practice. On one hand, there are families

who come to us in circumstances where organization was a priority. Such situations lead to a very orderly and efficient process. However, for the person who became incapacitated or passed away who was not organized, the resulting situation is quite different. We now come to the observation of distraught family members handing over the plastic bags which we described above. After they leave, the real work begins. The contents of those plastic bags are typically emptied onto a large boardroom table where professional clerical staff will begin the long process of sifting through loose and unorganized papers. From these bags will emerge stock certificates, house deeds, cottage deeds, bankbooks, some being current and some being out of date. There is no methodology or organization to the contents of those plastic bags. No one knows if the estate consists only of what is on that boardroom table or whether there are resources outside which have to be investigated. Quite often, the spouse or children will have a rough idea, but not a precise idea as to the full story. They might mention the possibility of bank accounts in another State, or a property in another country, or the possibility of further assets in the same State. They might make reference to money which is owed to the estate. However, where the breadwinner has kept all of the vital information to himself or herself, leaving his or her spouse and his or her children in the dark, one must realize that there is a serious likelihood that some of the assets which that breadwinner worked so hard to acquire during his or her lifetime will never be found.

When you read about the possibility of the spouse and children being disoriented and at the mercy of strangers and professionals, it is often disorganization which has put them in such an unenviable position.

In the type of situation which we have just described, your spouse and your children will be obliged to acquire knowledge and understanding of your financial situation in a relatively short period of time. It is in stressful situations of this nature that one of your family members can begin to blame another for overlooking something or miscommunicating something. That in itself is a source of stress and divisiveness within the family. In addition, the division of labor may not be looked upon by all of the family members as equitable. Some may feel that they are carrying the full load and that others are getting "a free ride" on their efforts. Again, the source of this type of tension can be traced back to disorganization.

You do not want to be disorganized when it comes to your financial affairs. So what can you do to organize?

You should prepare an inventory of your assets and liabilities. Our years of practice have taught us that people tend to have assets in many places. If your assets are scattered, there is a greater risk that some of them will be overlooked. In fact, there is a possibility that you yourself might forget about an out of State bank account that you opened up some years ago. Imagine, then, how hard it will be for your children to know what you own, if you, yourself, are struggling with the same subject.

As a result of your incapacity or death, your loved ones are going to have to locate your bank accounts, your stocks, your bonds, your real estate, and your other assets. They will also have to contact the important people in your life, such as your lawyer, your accountant, your stockbroker, your insurance agent and your financial planner.

It is easy to procrastinate on the subject of organizing your financial affairs. Somehow you may feel that your lawyer and your accountant will be able to piece everything together. However, as we have seen, this approach is likely to create difficulties among your family members, expose them to excess effort and expense, and is possibly going to expose them to the risk that some of the assets that belong to you will never be located.

If you are organized, or, as a result of reading this, become organized, we should then focus attention upon your parents. Everything that you have read pertaining to yourself is also applicable to them.

We appreciate that a discussion with your parents about organizing their financial affairs in the manner which we are describing can prove to be a sensitive and delicate matter. However, you also have to appreciate that you may be one of the persons facing the task of putting the puzzle of your parents' financial affairs together after their illness or death. Once you can embark upon a discussion with your parents, you should definitely include an explanation to them as to how important it is that they take the time now to prepare a roadmap of their financial affairs. You can explain that such a roadmap will make all the difference when ultimately you will be called upon to look after things. The concept of a roadmap is also applicable to the relationship between life partners. The considerations to which we have made reference above, apply not only in the relationships between parents and child and husband and wife, but also between common law and same sex partners.

It is a fact of life that people will tend to scatter their assets. Of course, there are always reasons for doing this. Sometimes you want to get a better rate of interest on your investments, other times you want to deal with a certain financial institution for some but not all of your assets and other times you will simply want to spread your risk. All of this being said, you carry in your head a general image of what you own, backed up by paperwork, which you have filed in various places convenient to you. However, your knowledge of the assets and the location of this paperwork is personal, and you will take this knowledge with you to the grave. If you wish to make matters easier for your loved ones, you may consider a strategy where you begin to bundle some or all of your assets instead of scattering them.

What do we mean by "bundling"? The word describes a process where you organize your assets in such a way that they will be easier to find and easier to deal with. In other words, if you are holding a large portfolio of stock with a number of brokers and institutions, you might consider reducing this number to one or two. You would then identify the one or two brokers or institutions to your loved ones. Further examples of bundling consist of banking in one or two banks as opposed to banking in several institutions scattered throughout your city. Of course you should consider utilizing the most convenient and the strongest of those institutions, bearing in mind, that you will want to take advantage of the best interest rates available. If you receive checks on a regular basis from a number of sources, such as interest on deposits, dividends from stocks or government pensions, you should consider directing all of these payments to one or two checking accounts in the one or two institutions which you have selected, so that the checks are automatically deposited in those accounts. Proceeding in this fashion should avoid loss of checks in the mail and also avoid the possibility that a check will arrive at your house, become overlooked and never deposited.

At this stage, another negative example will show how valuable it is to consider bundling as opposed to scattering assets. We speak of a real-life situation which has nothing to do with any legal matters. It is a simple story about a family who dealt for years with one video rental outlet. Matters were quite easy. Any member of the family, who wished to take out or to return a movie, simply took it out or returned it. There was never any problem. Any cassette would be put on the hall table and whoever would be passing by the video store would know that he or she would just pop the cassette in the return box at the video store. One day, all of this changed when our friend's spouse became innovative and started to rent movies from a second video rental outlet. You can probably guess the rest of this story. Before very long, a situation arose where our friend picked up the cassette off of the hall table and of course returned it to the original video outlet instead of the new video outlet. Several days later the new video outlet called our friend's spouse to ask for the return of the video. The spouse said that the video had already been returned. Five arguments and fifty dollars later, our friend came to the conclusion that what he had returned to the original video store was the cassette coming from the second video store. This very simple story is a good illustration of the type of risk that you expose yourself to if your assets are scattered too widely.

RECORD KEEPING CHECKLIST

Proper record keeping, pertaining to your life situation, both financial and otherwise, will greatly help your loved ones in the event of your incapacity or death. We hope that the following checklist will be of assistance to you in your efforts to become organized:

- The location or locations of all of the financial institutions with which you are dealing;

- The name, address and telephone number of your employer, or if you are self-employed, of your partners and business associates;
- The location of your birth and marriage certificates;
- The name of your stock broker;
- The name of your accountant;
- The name of your lawyer;
- The location of your file copies of tax returns which you filed with the government: This will be of great assistance to those who process your tax return after you pass away;
- The name and address of each of the companies which have issued credit cards to you, together with your account numbers; where you are dealing with a company which issues benefits, bonuses, points or any similar accommodation to their customers, you should specify any additional serial numbers and telephone contact numbers for redemption purposes; if the card is a gold card or similar type  of card which bears life insurance on any balance owing, you should include information which will alert those who survive you to the fact that the balance owing under such card is life insured;
- In the event you were adopted, the location of your adoption papers;
- In the event that your name was changed under process of law, the location of the documentation evidencing your change of name;
- In the event that you are divorced, the location of the original Divorce Judgment or Decree;

- In the event that your estate or any particular beneficiary is entitled to a death benefit, the location of the life insurance policy or other document generating such benefit. With respect to insurance, you should provide the addresses and telephone numbers of the brokers and insurance companies involved and the provision of a memo to whoever is looking after your estate specifying that they are to keep the insurance current and in force on your home, your car and your other valuable assets in the event that you have become incapacitated or pass away;

- The location of your safety deposit box specifying the address of the bank or financial institution and the specific location of the safety deposit box key;

- List all of the real estate which you own, either alone or together with any other party. Specify where property is held in joint venture arrangements, through corporations or syndicates, and specify property even if it is held out of the State and out of the country. In the event that there are any mortgages or leases pertaining to the property, specify that as well and specify whether there is any life insurance payable upon your death which could eliminate a mortgage loan on any of such property. These considerations include time share property;

- If you own or lease a motor vehicle your papers should be kept together with the proper evidence of insurance. The representative of your estate may be well advised to buy back a leased vehicle if there is equity in it at the time of your death. This would allow your representative to re-sell the vehicle at a profit and your estate would benefit accordingly;

- The location of any post office boxes in your name or in the name of your company;

- In the event that you are carrying on a partnership or have interest in a corporation, specify the name of the partnership or corporation and the location of minute books and incorporating documents. Specify the location of any partnership agreements or shareholders agreements which you may have, applicable to such business endeavors;

• Identify your Social Security Number and if you do have a Social Security Card, identify where it can be found;

• The location of your Durable Powers of Attorney for Property and for Health Care and any trust documentation or agreements which you may have, and you should list the names, addresses and telephone numbers of those whom you have appointed on these documents;

• The location of your prepaid funeral plan documentation;

• The location of your original Will, and any original Codicils to it. The location of any memo that you have prepared for the purpose of guiding your executor or guardian. It will be very helpful to provide the names, addresses and telephone numbers of all executors, guardians and witnesses to your Will and witnesses to any Codicils to your Will;

• In the event that you owe any money, specify particulars, including names, addresses and telephone numbers, and also specify whether the creditor has taken out any insurance in the event of your death, and whether the creditor has offered any form of reduction on payment of the debt. In the latter case, it would be valuable to gather evidence of such reduction while you are still alive and in good health because your representatives may have great difficulty in proving evidence of such reduction if you are incapacitated or have passed away.

• In the event that you are paying down a debt on a current basis, it would be helpful to provide on going evidence, such as check numbers or the dates of bank debits showing that no payments have been missed. This will avoid a creditor asking for more money than the creditor is entitled to. While you may not be able to maintain this kind of information on a monthly basis, it should at least be examined periodically, perhaps on your birthday each year. If you do have a loan with a bank or other financial institution, specify the name, address, telephone number and loan number allocated to your loan by the institution, and if available, the name and telephone number of your account representative. You should also specify the monthly payment;

•   In the event anyone owes you money, you should gather the original evidence of that debt such as an I.O.U., promissory note, or other evidence showing why the money is owed. As well, if you are being paid by post dated checks, identify where the post dated checks can be found. This would apply to anyone who owes you money including another family member. In the event that you are operating a small business, where you are monitoring the accounts receivable, you should specify where the accounts receivable are kept and keep the evidence of accounts receivable up to date and prepare them so that your representative can easily keep track of what is owing;

•   If you are operating a small business, and intend that your representatives keep it operating after you become incapacitated or pass away, you should itemize certain information critical to the operation of that business. Such information, for example, would consist of the addresses and telephone numbers of the key suppliers, the banker, the lawyer, the accountant, the insurance agent and other parties who have an important role to play in the operation of the business. In addition, you should record other information such as particulars of any trade shows, names of marketing agents you have dealt with, advertising and promotional contacts who are important, and similar important persons. You should prepare a file containing all of such matters which would allow your representatives to maintain the business as well as possible under the circumstances;

• Maintain, as best as possible, a detailed and up to date list of your assets, including all investments, stocks, mutual funds, certificates of deposit, treasury bills, and other similar types of investment. In all cases you should specify account numbers, the location of the institutions where they are kept or from where they are being administered including account representative names, telephone numbers, etc. You should also specify the location of any certificates in your possession, and if those certificates are in the possession of a broker, how to contact that broker. If you own stock, you should record the original purchase price of the stock. In the event that the stock either increases or decreases in value, the increase or decrease may have tax implications and your representative will find it much easier to do the calculations if the acquisition price of the stock were to be recorded;

• Specify whether your home, your office, your cottage, your condominium or any other real estate in your ownership, possession or control has an alarm system, and if so, set out the code so that your family will be able to shut the alarm off or put it on as the case may be;

• Record all of your access codes for automobile and garage door entry, computer passwords, etc. If there are any cards in your possession for garage door or office building entry, record the location of such cards;

• If you have recently acquired audiovisual equipment, computer equipment, or anything else which carries a manufacturer's or supplier's warranty, it would make sense to package all of the warranty material together with purchase receipts and specify where these are kept. If the warranties have expired, get rid of the paper;

• Record those of your personal items which you have loaned to other people. Examples would be an expensive lawn mower, power tools, etc.

It would be appropriate to make a few comments about this list. To begin with, some estates will require a more detailed and extensive checklist while other estates may be dealt with more simply. Secondly, the list should be made user friendly to your family. While many of us may manage with small bits of paper and items in our memory, this method is not going to be easy for your family to deal with if you are overtaken by a tragedy. You may have your own little pieces of paper and you may understand where your things are and you may know what you own. You may also know who your important people are. But how do you know that all of this information is going to get to your children or your spouse or others who love you? What you have to do is to make sure that they will be prepared to act if and when the time comes. Perhaps it would be a good idea to sit down with your family and discuss all of the items on this checklist, and to confirm who your professional representatives are. In addition to this type of discussion, you should also do the very best you can to organize in a business like and efficient manner. You should not have to go far to find the format that is most workable for you. Certainly, you should not have to go any further than a reading of the organizational and estate planning books in your local library or your office supply store. A discussion with your insurance agent and your financial planner will also be helpful. These are all vehicles which will lead you to a proper organized format.

Now that we have seen the advantage of organizing your financial affairs, let us turn our attention to additional efforts which can help to eliminate stress and the potential for family conflict if and when in the future you lose your ability to express those wishes to your family.

It is a good idea to write what we might call a wish list so that you are able to speak to your loved ones through your written memo in the event of your incapacity or death. A wish list can be of great assistance to your family. It can provide a sense of comfort to your loved ones. Remember that your wish list is not a legal document and is therefore not binding on anyone. It cannot take precedence over your Will. It will help to guide your children and make life easier for them. For example, if your wish list makes it very clear that you wanted one child to receive the family album, the painting in your living room, a war medal or other similar personal items, the fact that you have a written memorandum setting out your wishes is going to go a long way to soothe the feelings of other family members who did not receive these personal items. Some of the biggest fights in an estate may occur over personal items, such as a sterling silver tray or a family heirloom.

If you are a parent of young children, you might even express some of your heartfelt wishes to your appointed guardian, which can relate to the lifestyle and upbringing of your young children. In fact, you can look upon a memo of this nature or even an audio or video tape as a method of speaking to your loved ones after you are no longer able to do so, either in the case of incapacity or death. Communication of this nature will allow a loved one to accept a gift which you left in your Will without a sense of guilt and without a sense that he or she may be taking something away that another child wanted. In the same light, you may recall Yul Brenner doing an anti-cigarette commercial which he wanted played after his death. He intended to have a serious impact on those watching his commercial, which was anti-smoking. It did in fact have a significant impact on many people, because it was played after he had passed away. Similarly, a letter, audio tape or a video tape which you prepare to be read or heard or seen after your death will similarly have a heavy impact upon your loved ones. To  emphasize again for the purposes of this discussion, we are talking about the non-binding expression of your wishes. Accordingly, you must remember that the letter, the audiotape and the videotape to which we are making reference will have no legal or binding effect upon your estate and they are not in any manner a replacement for your Will.

We have seen that a failure to properly organize will cause your family anxiety and frustration, all of which are probable causes of family conflict. We will now turn our attention to another source of difficulty which can also bring a family into conflict. Let us examine some problems arising from planning based upon inappropriate assumptions.

PLANNING BASED UPON INAPPROPRIATE ASSUMPTIONS

Many people are tempted to base their planning upon preconceived notions and assumptions. We might comment that following such a path can lead, sooner or later, to conflict within your family. Let us examine some assumptions which should not be used as the foundation of your planning:

1. Do not assume that you have completed your estate planning once you have signed your Will. You will recall from our previous discussion that your Will is only one aspect of your estate planning. You will also recall our discussion with respect to incapacity. Your Will is effective when you die, but will not help you if, while you are still alive, you lose your mental capacity, either through an accident or an illness. To protect yourself against that sort of a situation, you will require the Durable Power of Attorney for Property and the Durable Power of Attorney for Health Care which we previously spoke about. Without these documents, your family may have to go to court in order to be able to act for you if you become mentally incapable. The discussion does not end there. You must also consider advice on whom to name as beneficiaries in your life insurance policies. Furthermore, you should also be taking advice as to whether you should have joint ownership with your loved ones on bank accounts, your family home or other assets.

2. Do not assume that a parent will outlive a child. In our practice, we have seen situations where children have passed away, leaving grieving parents. To make matters worse, many young adults do not contemplate an untimely death, and if that tragedy overtakes them, they leave an estate which is devoid of preparation or planning, yielding unwelcome and unforeseen problems for their distraught parents.

3. Do not assume that your child's marriage will be permanent. It would appear that the divorce rate is relatively high compared to what it was in earlier decades and as a result, marital breakdown must be a consideration in your planning, no matter how remote or painful the thought may be. With this in mind, you might consider whether it is practical to appoint your daughter-in-law or your son-in-law as a backup executor in your Will, as a backup attorney in your Durable Power of Attorney for Property,

or as a backup attorney in your Durable Power of Attorney for Health Care. Remember that once you become incapacitated or you pass away, you will no longer be able to change any of the above documents. This could result in a situation where your separated daughter-in law or separated son-in-law is looking after your affairs if you become incapacitated or you die.

4. Do not assume that all of your beneficiaries will be able to inherit, or will want to inherit a particular asset that you own. The first example that comes to mind would consist of a widow who has a daughter and a son. The widow leaves her condominium to her daughter, who happens to have both children and pets. The widow never considered that her own condominium was governed by by-laws which prohibited both children and pets. When the widow ultimately passes away, the daughter inherits an asset which is going to bring her into conflict with a hostile Board of Directors. This could force her to sell the condominium. On the other hand, imagine that the widow's son might have been able to take this same condominium without breaking any by-laws. The moral of this story is to acquire intimate knowledge of both the asset and the life circumstances of the beneficiary to whom the asset is being left, as part of your Will planning.

We have seen a situation where a child may wish to inherit a particular asset, but is for various reasons unable to take owner-ship or possession of it. Now let us look at an example of a child who is able to own or possess the asset, but who does not wish to do so. This example would consist of leaving the shares in your business to a child, without fully discussing with that child, the implications of that gift. Suppose for example your business raises environmental issues, in circumstances where you are leaving your shares in that business to a child who may have a very negative reaction to the type of business in which you were involved.

We can envisage yet another problem arising in terms of giv-ing shares in a business to a child under your Will. This time, your child is perfectly willing to take the shares in your business, but those shares are subject to a shareholders' agreement which compels your estate to sell your shares to your co- shareholders, who have a right of first refusal. You can assume that your co-shareholders will fight aggressively to keep your child from getting involved in the business, if it is in their own best interests to do so.

We have just seen three examples of situations which arise where parents pick out assets to give to their children without giving adequate consideration to whether the child is willing or able to accept that gift.

5. Do not assume that your beneficiaries will always have the best of intentions. Imagine that you have two children, one of whom works for a large corporation and is not subject to any business risks. Your second child, on the contrary, is a business person who has exposed himself to significant creditor guarantees. His future is bright, provided that his business continues to succeed. However, in a downturn, your second child faces a real possibility of suffering a serious financial setback. Knowing this, you come to the logical conclusion that if your estate is equally divided between the two children, the second child may lose most of what you have to leave. In order to avoid such a loss, you make the assumption that if you leave everything to the first child, you can rely upon the goodwill of that first child to distribute one half of what you leave to the second child.

However, this assumption is a weak one:

• you are assuming, perhaps incorrectly, that the first child has the good intentions toward his sibling that you expect that child to have;

- even if the first child has a heart of gold, his spouse may be aggressive, domineering and will not quietly part with anything within her grasp;
- what if your child has a heart of gold and his spouse has a heart of gold, but shortly after your death, both the first child and his spouse pass away leaving children (your grandchildren) whose only intention is to extend their reach to every legal asset within their grasp, notwithstanding any moral obligations to an uncle.

In all three instances, we have a situation where the estate plan is based upon dangerous assumptions.

Although there may be some families where you can deviate from the legal position, it is certainly not advisable to do so, given the problems which can arise in the way we have described them above.

6. Do not assume that one of your children wants to be your sole executor to the exclusion of his or her siblings. In fact, that particular child whom you wanted may not have the time to devote and may in fact strongly desire that his or her siblings be appointed along with him or her.

7. Do not assume that when you die you are only going to have what you own today. Remember, assets grow. You may win a lottery, etc. There may be inheritances coming to you from family members. As well, your assets can deplete, so if you are thinking of leaving a sum of money to a particular person, make sure that that amount will be there when you die.

8. Do not assume that your children from your first marriage will get along with your second spouse after your death. Your second spouse is not the parent of those children. Those children may harbor a fear that after you pass away, your spouse will revise his or her Will and completely cut them out. In order to protect the children from your first marriage without upsetting the relationship with your second spouse, you should speak to your lawyer about various options regarding second marriage estate planning.

9. Do not assume that because you hold all of your assets jointly with right of survivorship, with your spouse, that you do not need a Will. What happens if both you are your spouse die in an accident? The assets may flow from husband to wife or from wife to husband, but they certainly do not flow any further under these arrangements. In order to pass the assets to a child or another beneficiary, you will be best served by having a Will in place as part of your planning.

10. Do not assume that the assets in your estate will be enough to cover your debts and your taxes. Many people consider obtaining life insurance which names their estate as beneficiary. Such life insurance is there in order to fund debts and taxes, which may prove to be substantial. Debts and taxes must get paid before any beneficiaries can take their entitlement.

11. Do not assume that you can carry out all of your estate planning on your own without the help of experts in the field. Internet information, newspaper and magazine articles and generic advice are helpful, but do not address variances between the laws of different States, and certainly do not address your own particular, unique situation.

12. Do not assume that if you are separated from your spouse, a simple change to your Will is going to prevent that spouse from benefiting from your estate. What if you appointed him or her as beneficiary in an insurance policy or pension plan? What if you and your separated spouse owned a property jointly with right of survivorship? Under these circumstances, your separated spouse may benefit despite your attempts to deal with his or her entitlement by making changes to your Will. We cannot emphasize enough how important it is to discuss matters of this nature with your lawyer if it is your intention that your separated spouse derive no benefit from your estate.

INHERITING TURMOIL–
REAL LIFE EXAMPLES

In our practice, we find that many of the clients who discuss their needs with us tend to open up after a while and as a result, over the years, we have become a repository of many stories experienced by people of varying ages, in various walks of life. In addition to the stories we have been told, we have of course seen situations unfold as part of our legal practice, and we have become upfront observers of family members fighting with each other.

There are many instances where misunderstandings and miscommunications create minor issues among family members. Such minor issues can, quite often, be remedied by apologies and explanations. However, there are far too many instances where apologies and explanations are simply not enough to resolve what becomes a very deep and lasting conflict. It is this form of turmoil that we wish to address here. We have not only heard about, but have also personally witnessed, unfortunate situations arising between siblings, between parents and their children, between certain grandchildren and other grandchildren and between uncles and aunts on the one hand, and their nephews and nieces on the other. In addition, we have seen stressful relationships between the children of a first marriage on one hand, and the spouse of the second or third marriage on the other.

Up to this point, we have been providing general guidance on the subject of avoiding conflicts within your family. However, it is now time to relate what we have actually seen and heard in real life terms. Hopefully, the observations that we are about to pass on to you will not  only serve to illustrate how important it is to put thought into your planning, but will also serve as something that you can pass on to others so that everyone can learn from mistakes of the past. That having been said, let us pass on to a series of sad and touching stories which are part of the repository to which we have made reference above. In addition to those stories, we will also add some observations which have come to us, partly from our day to day practice and partly from what some members of the public have told us when we have appeared as guests on radio and television shows. Preserving the lawyer's obligations of confidentiality, the names of the parties, the places where the events took place and the timing of those events have all been omitted from these stories. As we previously indicated, we are of the view that these will serve a solid educational purpose.

Our first story starts off with one very simple image, being that of an empty chair. According to our client, that empty chair was situated at Table 5 at our client's wedding. In order to have you in the lawyer's office with us as this sad story unfolds, it is best to travel back in time to see how the seeds of this tragedy were sown. Very shortly, you will see why the empty chair at that table was of such significance to our client at her wedding. You see, that chair is where her beloved Aunt Joan should have been sitting in order to help celebrate our client's wedding. Sitting at the head table, our client kept staring at that empty chair and she was so hurt that the pain had stayed with her and was deep enough that she felt a need to unburden herself to us when she was in our office. You see, our client was extremely close to her Aunt Joan for many years and our client could not get past the fact that Joan did not come to her wedding. You may ask at this point what events could have caused the destruction of such a close relationship between an Aunt and her niece? According to our client, this is the story:

In simple terms, let us look at Aunt Joan and her brother Steven. Steven was our client's father. Joan and Steven themselves were very close until their mother (our client's grandmother) had a stroke and required a full-time caregiver. According to our client, Steven and Joan decided that for the meantime, Joan would be the caregiver and Steven would go on to pursue his education. Joan lived with her mother and continued her caregiving right up until the time that her mother passed away. The caregiving role that Joan took on lasted many years and our client was forever grateful and respectful of Joan for sacrificing her own lifestyle to live with and care for her mother. Meanwhile, our client's father, Steven, moved on with his life. Steven's life was

complete with a university education, a happy marriage, children (of which our client was one) and a flourishing professional career. To our client, it was commonly understood among the family members that when grandmother would pass away, Joan would get the house in return for the sacrifices she had made over so many years. However, this may well have been a common understanding among the family, but the reality was that grandmother left a Will and divided her estate equally between Joan and Steven. The Will did not grant to Joan, the special recognition that Joan had expected: In other words, the Will did not leave the house to Joan. No one can speculate what was in grandmother's mind. Did she really expect that Steven would voluntarily give the house to his sister? The answer to that question will never be known. When all of this became known to our client, her own reaction was to attempt to persuade her father, Steven, to do the right thing and to release his interest in that home. Nothing could persuade Steven to release anything. He apparently had his own financial requirements, retained a lawyer, and adamantly insisted on enforcing all of his rights under his mother's Will. Our client never received any feedback from her Aunt Joan, and our client at that time, had no way of measuring the effect that her father's decision had upon Aunt Joan: at least, not until our client's wedding day. Aunt Joan simply did not show up. That is why the chair at Table 5 remained empty.

This story describes some very deep wounds which in the end affected our client, an innocent and sympathetic bystander to the breakup between a brother and a sister. And what can we learn from this? Fairness is dictated by the circumstances in your family, and you cannot simply stamp an equal sign on your affairs and walk away. Certainly, according to our client, she has no doubt in her mind that her aunt felt very much taken advantage of by the family's failure to recognize her sacrifices over so many years.

As we move on from our first story, you might turn your thoughts to those parents who for various reasons find it inappropriate or uncomfortable to discuss matters of this nature with their children. Perhaps it is a function of superstition, procrastination, or maybe the parent has always been tightlipped and kept matters to himself or herself. But the reality is that your family may pay a huge price for this culture of secrecy. This unwillingness to communicate with the family leads us to the next series of stories.

Two brothers came into our office shortly after the death of their father. It was obvious from their demeanour that the relationship between them was quite strained. Knowing these clients from previous dealings, we were more than surprised at the coldness between them, because they had always been close before their father passed away. Furthermore, the Will left everything equally to them, named both of them as executors and the estate itself was not large. Initially, we were baffled at what could possibly cause such a change in their attitudes towards each other. The answer came out slowly, and after a number of meetings involved in settling the estate. In this case, their father never discussed his funeral or burial wishes with either of his sons because he believed in keeping these matters to himself. One of the brothers wished to have an elaborate funeral while the other, who was the domineering one, wanted a very simple one on the grounds that the less money spent, the greater the inheritance. In the end, it was the domineering brother who got his way, but in getting his way, he created strain, hard feelings and disruption between brothers who had previously been considerably closer than they now were. The son

who gave in made a point of telling us in his brother's presence how great a man his father was and how deserving he was of proper treatment at his death. He went on to express how guilty he felt in shortchanging the proper recognition his father deserved. Meanwhile, the domineering son sat in silence and it was evident that these two brothers would have to take enormous efforts to regain the good relationship they had enjoyed before their father passed away. Our own reaction is quite simple: If only their father had discussed his funeral and burial wishes with his sons, it is most likely that the acrimony and strain to which we were witness would never have occurred.

We now come to two further stories, where the same type of lack of communication affects a family in the context of a parent's incapacity as opposed to a parent's death.

The first of our two stories involves a mother who did not plan ahead by leaving a proper Durable Power of Attorney for Health Care and a Living Will. By failing to arrange for these documents, she left no guidance to her two adult daughters which would otherwise have told them what to do if it became necessary to look after her. As you may recall from previous discussions in this book, these documents are very important. Through these documents you can appoint someone to carry out your wishes in circumstances where you will be unable to make medical decisions for yourself because of your own incapacity. These documents will also allow you to express your wishes regarding your personal and medical care. Furthermore, through these documents, you can express what you wish to be done in the event that you are gravely ill or seriously injured in circumstances where there is no realistic hope of your recovery.

In the case at hand, since the mother did not prepare the documentation to which we have made reference in the last paragraph, the law gave both of her daughters the power to make medical decisions of this nature for her. However, the situation was not quite that simple. In this case, neither daughter knew what their mother wanted, and their mother was no longer capable of expressing her wishes because of her incapacity. Our client was one of those two daughters. She wanted more than anything that her mother would avoid pain and suffering. On the other hand, her sister felt that every effort should be made to prolong her mother's life as long as possible and at any cost. It is worth repeating that the mother left no instructions on this point. You will very shortly see that as honorable as these motivations sound, they brought the two sisters on a collision course with each other. Ultimately, their mother passed away, but what we are addressing here relates to a ten-day period of agony, which our client felt her mother could have and should have avoided. The agony, without getting into too much detail, was evident to my client because although her mother was incommunicative, our client could detect the tension and the sweat on her mother's face when her mother was in pain. It was common knowledge among our client, her sister and the doctor that intermittent administration of morphine would be consistent with prolonging their mother's life to a greater extent than would the administration of constant morphine without interruption. Our client wished to ease her mother's pain. Her sister wished to prolong her mother's life. After a significant argument, our client's sister had her way and the program became one of administering morphine on an intermittent basis. This situation brought tension between the two sisters and the relationship between them deteriorated and became damaged. Although this is not a case where litigation was contemplated, it was a case where a proper Durable Power of Attorney for Health Care and Living Will would have given the necessary medical directives. Those directives would have gone a long way to avoid the strained relationship between the two sisters.

This brings us to a second story which involves a failure of a parent to communicate with her children. This story involves a

Durable Power of Attorney for Property, and it is told to us by one of three adult children who lives in the same city as her mother. Her other two siblings live in a different city. In this case, due to a lack of communication between the mother and her three children, the mother appointed our client alone to represent her as her attorney under a Durable Power of Attorney for Property. It was only after her mother had become incapacitated, that our client first realized that she was the sole appointee under that Durable Power of Attorney for Property. At that stage, according to our client, she was quite taken by surprise, and could only speculate that her mother had named her as sole attorney and excluded her sisters, because our client happened to have lived in the same city as her mother, and her sisters did not.

The incapacity prevented any discussion between our client and her mother on the subject of adding her two siblings as co-attorneys under the Durable Power of Attorney for Property. Now that her mother is incapacitated, our client tells us of the stress and burden imposed upon her in looking after all of her mother's financial affairs. Meanwhile, our client's siblings have been offended at not having been named on the Power of Attorney and they have now turned their backs on the situation. Our client went on to quote one of her siblings as having said "Mom named you – you do it all". Our client, of course, is worried because if she makes one wrong move, her siblings will criticize her. This situation is further aggravated because our client has asked her siblings for help and they have refused. Our client, meanwhile has to look after her own family and maintains a full time job. The additional tasks imposed under the Durable Power of Attorney for Property have created quite a burden for our client. In addition, it is evident from what our client has told us that her relationship with her siblings has deteriorated. This story shows once again what can happen where a parent fails to discuss a matter of this nature with his or her children. Based upon the narrative of our client, we are left with the impression, for better or for worse, that the only consideration involved in the mother's appointment of her daughter was geography. If indeed that was the reasoning of the mother, her logic was entirely inappropriate, and resulted in straining the relationship among her children.

You may have the best intentions in the world, but unless those intentions are expressed clearly and with precision in a Will, you are creating a risk that your family might come up with two different versions of your true intentions and this can express itself in a family dispute.

Everyone is well advised to retain a lawyer for the purpose of preparing his or her last Will. Those who fail to recognize the need for precise wording in a Will may be tempted to save money and create a homemade Will. However, this kind of saving very often proves to be illusory. If a homemade Will is capable of being interpreted two different ways, you will in all likelihood have two different family members asserting two different claims and thereby generating costs and bitterness which vastly exceed what you saved by failing to spend money on a lawyer. On top of the monetary costs, come the heart-breaking costs of tearing a family apart.

One could safely assume that many people have prepared home-made Wills. One might wonder why most homemade Wills are different from Wills prepared by lawyers. What we have seen might very briefly be summarized as a failure to use precise language and a failure to recognize those contingencies which might arise if events unfold in a pattern different from what the layperson contemplated in the course of drafting his or her Will. To illustrate the need for precise wording in a Will, one need not go much further than to examine a case involving a homemade Will, which was decided in court. In that particular case, there was a fight between various beneficiaries over a number of issues, most of which had to be dealt with by the court. Within those issues, one of the most dramatic questions that had to be determined pertained to a gift expressed in the following clause:

"My personal monies at the time of my death are to be divided equally between my four sisters and one brother as follows: ...."

Although the wording sounds logical, it was capable of two interpretations. One group of litigants argued that wording should only include the two bank accounts which belonged to the deceased. The other group of litigants argued that the term "My personal monies" should refer not only to the two bank accounts, but also to investment certificates, term deposits and other securities. After considerable fighting, and very detailed and lengthy court reasoning, the court decided to place itself into the shoes of the person making the Will at the time that the Will was made. Based upon that reasoning, the court decided that the term "My personal monies" was restricted to the two bank accounts and to no other assets. It is noteworthy that the litigants consisted, on the one hand, of the deceased's husband, who argued that the term "My personal monies" should only include the two bank accounts belonging to the deceased, and on the other hand, the deceased's siblings, who argued that the term "My personal monies" referred not only to the two bank accounts, but also to investment certificates, term deposits and other securities. It is a certainty that the costs of this court fight vastly exceeded the savings that the deceased had pocketed by doing her own Will without the advice of a professional. Perhaps, however, the monetary costs are the minor result created by the homemade Will. The major problem is likely to be the hostility and acrimony, which it is logical to assume, will forever cloud the relationship between the husband of the deceased and her siblings.

The case we have just described is a mere illustration of the problems which can result by imprecise language in a Will. Before we mentioned this case, we made note that imprecise language is not the only difficulty to be found in a layperson's Will. The failure to recognize contingencies which may occur represents another problem to be found in homemade Wills. Before going to another story, which will illustrate a failure to consider contingencies in the preparation of a homemade Will, we should point out one other problem which has not been touched upon so far. If no professional is involved, there is a real danger that the Will may be improperly witnessed and improperly signed. We have seen circumstances where a homemade Will bore no signature at all. However, at this point let us progress to the next story.

A young man came to our office to seek advice as to whether he had any claim against the estate of his late grandfather. In seeking this advice from us, he first showed us a copy of the homemade Will which his grandfather had made and which had ultimately come into the hands of our client. The Will was a very old homemade one, prepared at a time when our client's grandfather had only one grandchild and it was not our client. The Will left that grandchild the sum of $150,000.00. As matters turned out, our client's grandfather never again prepared another Will, notwithstanding that our client was born during the ensuing years. Our client became very close with his grandfather over the course of time, and it was inconceivable to our client that his grandfather would cut him out of his Will, while naming his cousin. According to the reasoning of our client, he felt that something should be done to reflect the true feelings of his grandfather. We had the unfortunate task of advising our client that no one will ever know the true feelings of his grandfather because all we are left with is the Will, which very clearly stated that our client would receive absolutely nothing. One can only speculate as to what was in the mind of his grandfather over the many years. One might suppose that the grandfather simply forgot to review his Will, but that is only speculation. What we are left with is the bare fact that our client was devastated in having been cut out of his grandfather's Will and it is doubtful that he will ever understand why. On the assumption that the grandfather felt as our client thought he felt, the story might have had a much happier conclusion. The grandfather would have sought legal advice, and in all likelihood the lawyer would have discussed with the grandfather, the possibility of future grandchildren. It would be reasonable to expect that the grandfather would then have prepared a new Will which accurately reflected his feelings.

Let us turn to another story relating to problems resulting from the language used in a homemade Will. A client of our firm consulted us because he was encountering a serious dispute over very expensive house-hold items which his second wife's children wished to remove from the household after his second wife passed away. This curious dispute arose from the following situation.  After our client's first wife passed away, he remarried a woman who had two sons. Our client purchased his current home with his second wife and over the course of their marriage, they furnished the home quite lavishly. The problem arose from the homemade Will that his second wife prepared. In her homemade Will, she left the household goods to her sons, obviously never contemplating what would happen if she predeceased our client. She simply never addressed this situation. Since the home was held jointly between our client and his second wife, our client naturally became the owner of the home when she died. The problem was that the contents of the home did not flow with the ownership of the real estate. She left the contents to her sons as stated above, and they were simply exercising their legal rights under the Will that she left. To add to the problem, certain items in the home in fact belonged to her alone, while other items in the home were jointly acquired by both husband and wife. Still other items were owned by our client alone. The matter has become acrimonious. There is currently a hostile relationship between our client and his two stepchildren and our client has expressed his disbelief that the wording in his wife's Will could create such a nightmare.

We will now turn to yet another homemade Will story, this time relating to business assets. From time to time, we have appeared as guest speakers on radio call-in shows, for the purpose of discussing various ways of minimizing family disputes. Some time ago, after one of our shows, we received a call from a young man who wanted to tell us how the once warm relationships in his family were destroyed because his wealthy father did not feel it was necessary to consult a lawyer for the purpose of preparing his Will. The young man's story will show how oversights in planning can lead to the nightmare to which we make reference over and over again. Among the very many assets which his father held, was the bowling alley which the young man managed for many years. It made sense that when his father passed away, the young man was the one who inherited the bowling alley. What upset the young man about this inheritance was that the young man's siblings were also his landlords. The young man is convinced that his father never intended this situation to occur, and he blames his father's failure to obtain proper advice in setting up the estate that he left. Now let us examine how this arose.

Many years ago, his father owned the bowling alley, together with the land and the building upon which it was situated. However, from the recollection of the young man, his father received tax saving advice and put the bowling alley business in one company and put the land and the building in another company. Having created that distinction, the father trivialized it when he created his Will on his own. You see, in putting the young man's story together, it was evident that his father had given the shares in the bowling alley company to his son, and evidently must have forgotten to give the shares in the land and the building to his son as well. The shares in the company that owned the land and the building went generally to all of the children equally, putting the young man in a minority position within that general gift. For these reasons, the young man now has to deal with his siblings as landlords. We might say that the young man had no hesitation in indicating to us that the increases in rent for the bowling alley were unreasonable, disproportionate to the marketplace and without any semblance of compassion for the young man's ability to make a living. He also took the trouble to point out his belief that this mean spirited approach was driven as much by the spouses of his siblings as by the siblings themselves. He left us with the impression that the entire situation was poisoned and that the family would never see eye to eye again.

The next story relates to preparation of a Will in a vacuum. What we mean to say when we refer to a vacuum is a failure of the person making the Will to appreciate what he or she will own at the time when he or she dies. There are planning steps which are sometimes misunderstood, such as putting property in joint ownership with right of survivorship or naming a beneficiary on a policy of insurance, and there are other examples of this type of strategy as well. Where these strategies are coordinated professionally, they constitute an excellent estate-planning tool. But when they are utilized without the proper knowledge or guidance, they can wreak havoc upon a family and this story illustrates how.

Our client was one of two daughters of a recently deceased widow. In her Will, our client's mother left her entire estate equally between our client and our client's sister. What brought our client to consult us was her anger surrounding the disposition of one of the largest assets that our client knew about, which consisted of a $20,000.00 bank account. That bank account was cleaned out by our client's sister very shortly after their mother passed away and our client was extremely dissatisfied when given the reason for this occurrence. Upon looking into this matter, we found that the bank account in question was held jointly between our client's mother and our client's sister. Our client had asked her sister for half of the proceeds of that account, only to meet with a refusal. Our client argues that it was obviously the intention of her mother to distribute that account equally between her and her sister. Our client argues that the reason her mother put the account in joint names with her sister was because it was convenient for her mother to do so in view of the fact that her sister lived so close to her mother and could help her mother with the banking. Our client is adamant that her mother never understood the true meaning of a joint bank account and our client is furious that her sister was taking advantage of her mother's ignorance. Our client felt so strongly that she almost accused her sister of stealing the money. Our client repeats over and over again her belief that her mother wanted that money split evenly as part of the estate. On reviewing this situation for our client, we did point out certain avenues that she could take, but she was loathe to become involved in the court system, and she was unprepared to invest the time, the money and the emotions for the purpose of advancing a claim against her sister. However, what our client did say is that she would never speak to her sister or her sister's family ever again.

We are going to turn to two stories relating to the appointment of executors. Before turning those stories over to you, we would like to take a moment to emphasize that the decision of appointing an executor is not one which should be trivialized. A poor choice of executor can cause extreme hardship and stress on your family if the decision is made without thinking through all of the implications of the appointment.

It is important to devote the time and the thought process necessary to establish a practical and workable appointment, because in choosing your executor, you are in fact conferring powers upon someone which will be used after you have passed away, and after you no longer have any ability to provide further input into the decision making process. Going further into this analysis, most people, after devoting thought to the matter, will appoint an executor for reasons which to them are logical and make sense. Some appointments result from the fact that the executor lives close at hand and that the convenience of a nearby executor is an overriding factor. Others will appoint an eldest child because the parent has the most confidence in that child by reason of his or her maturity. Still others may appoint the child who did very well in his accounting course. The parent may feel that such a child has a good head for business, good business instincts and will make a good executor. As good as these reasons may be, a question must still be answered: Will the appointment have any negative effects upon the family generally? True enough, no one can tell a person what to do in choosing his or her executor. However, it is also true that if your choice is made in haste or with inadequate consideration, the consequences can bring those whom you love and for whom you care into serious conflict with each other. With these thoughts in mind, let us now turn to our two executor selection stories.

In the first of our two stories, three adult children came to our office after their mother passed away. Her last Will named the eldest of the three children as executor. At first, when the three children came to our office, all three came into the boardroom and sat as equals. However, several minutes into that meeting, the child named as executor asked the other two children to leave the room. The executor indicated to us that he wished to discuss the matters of the forthcoming administration of the estate in privacy and without the involvement of his siblings. His status as sole executor, of course, gave him this power and the other two children immediately left the room. As they departed from the room, we could feel the air chill. It was evident to us that the siblings who had to leave, were not happy about it and felt in an inferior position to their brother. That was not the end of the story. Several days later, we received a call from one of these siblings. With fear in his voice, he said to us "I hope my brother does not sell the family cottage. He never uses it and may possibly consider selling it. But I would tell you, that to my sister and I, there is a lot of history and nostalgia connected with that cottage. If the estate needs the money, please let us know because we do not want it sold from under us. We know that he has the power to do it."

We will never know the reasons that their mother had for appointing one of the three children as sole executor. We can only guess that she felt comfortable with that particular child because he was the eldest. All three children were equal beneficiaries in the estate so that there was no question of favoritism in terms of distributing her assets. However, she gave power over the estate to one of her three children and that child exercised that power very visibly in front of the other two. We are led to wonder what the attitude of their mother would have been if she could have heard the fear in the voice of the child who called regarding preserving the family cottage.

This leads us to a more dramatic story which has come to our attention. The story begins very modestly, where we find the parents in their lawyer's office preparing their Wills. At the time, their son was in his early twenties and their two daughters were each in their early teens. In their Wills, the parents named each other as primary executors, and took the precaution of naming their son as backup executor. As the years passed, their children grew up and their fortunes changed. One of their young daughters became a doctor, the other became an engineer and the eldest son, as the story goes, became involved with substance abuse. When both parents subsequently passed away, in rapid succession, the son with the substance abuse problems remained as sole executor. From what we have heard, the son is absolutely insistent upon maintaining his power as executor, together with the compensation that goes along with it. We also understand that his siblings are adamantly opposed to his appointment, expressing concern that because of their brother's lifestyle, and his addictive problems, that the funds in the estate might be at risk of misuse or depletion. It is hard to come away from this story with a comfortable feeling. Unquestionably, the parents should have dealt with the issue of naming an executor in line with the radical change in the lifestyles of their children. If they had felt at all costs that their son should be named, they might have considered naming all three children, with the proviso that the vote of any two would be binding upon the estate.

Our next story brings us to another consideration: estate planning in a first marriage situation can be very different from second marriage estate planning. Our story will be of considerable interest to those who are in a second or subsequent marriage and have children.

Here is what a caller told us when we appeared as guests on a radio show: after his mother died, his father fell in love with another woman who had children from her prior marriage. The caller told us that he got along very well with both his father and his father's new wife. He was given to understand that when both his father and stepmother had passed away, he would receive one-third of the estate and the children of his stepmother would receive the other two-thirds. As it turned out, his father passed away before his stepmother, and his father's Will left everything to his stepmother. Our caller's surprise came when, several years after the death of his father, his stepmother passed away and her new Will left everything to her own children, cutting out the caller. Needless to say, the devastation and heartbreak that the caller had felt from all of this had led him to tell us this story. What was even more dramatic about his call to us, was the following consideration: the family heirlooms that had been passed to our caller's father were all transferred, lock, stock and barrel, to his stepmother under his father's Will. However, his stepmother was now leaving all of those heirlooms, not to our caller, but to her own children. Of course, the pain and heartbreak is not restricted to the family heirlooms. Along with those heirlooms came precious collections put together over many years, valuable real estate which had been passed down to his father through his family and, of course, stocks, bonds, bank accounts and other investments. In the end, everything that his father had acquired over the years was given to the stepsiblings of the caller, through the stepmother's Will. What led to this heartbreaking story lies in a series of assumptions that many people might make, which are mere assumptions and which do not result in protective planning. Apparently, the caller's father assumed that if he left everything to his second wife, she would look after his son in her own Will. The results of this story show how incorrect this assumption was. The caller did not hesitate to express his utter disappointment and frustration. Before terminating his call on the air, the caller made a point of expressing his bitterness and disgust over the fact that his stepsiblings would not relinquish one single item that was left to them, even though their windfall was a result of the lifelong efforts and hard work of our caller's father.

To this point, we have seen a number of situations involving lack of foresight or poor planning as they relate to the preparation of Wills and Powers of Attorney. The next and final story relates to the nightmare that can occur when a person passes away without a Will.

If in fact you pass away without a Will it is your State law that will determine who will inherit your estate. Furthermore, if there is no Will, there is no executor appointment, and since no executor has been appointed, someone will have to apply to administer your estate. Usually, this takes the form of a court appointment based upon the consent of all of the heirs. A further complication will arise where some of the heirs are incapable of giving their consent because they may be under age or they may have lost their mental capacity. As you might expect, all of this is likely to cause turmoil in the family. The following story illustrates such turmoil.

Some time ago, a gentleman approached our firm with a view to retaining us in the situation which we will now describe. He was one of seven siblings. Their parents had passed away long ago, and what brought him to our office was the recent decease of his sister. She died as a single woman without children, and left no Will. She also died without leaving any indication as to what her assets were or where they were located. You will shortly see from the rest of this narrative, that at the time of the death of their sister, all of the siblings had the impression that the assets of their recently deceased sister were substantial, but of all of the siblings, the only one who knew anything about these assets was their brother, the gentleman who initially contacted us. This particular gentleman told us of his feelings to the effect that he had earned the respect of his brothers and his sisters. He also told us that he himself took on the role of organizing the administration of the estate of his deceased sister for the benefit of all of the siblings. As a result of our initial meeting with him, he made arrangements to call all of his siblings to a gathering in our boardroom, where, figuratively speaking, all of the broken pieces of the estate would hopefully be put together and the family would organize for the purpose of taking some positive steps toward the administration of the estate of their recently deceased sister. The gentleman contemplated that organizing in this manner would make it easier to trace assets, gain credibility with banks and move on with the search for valuable assets.

We come now to the family meeting in the boardroom of our office. At that meeting you could cut the tension in the air with a knife. The two surviving sisters were convinced that their brother, the gentleman who had consulted us, was disclosing only part of the assets in the estate, and that he was hiding other assets from them. However, the gentleman's brothers had all the confidence in the world in him, essentially pitting brother against sister. Tensions mounted very rapidly. At one point, the sisters demanded that the gentleman open his briefcase to disclose the contents, and when he refused, the sisters became enraged. His refusal, as he rationalized it, was based upon the fact that the contents of his briefcase did not relate to this particular estate and that he did not want to disclose his personal affairs to the people in that room. As the tensions rose, the voices rose and it was not long before there were insults, screaming, offensive gestures, and at one point, one of the brothers threw a pad of paper against the wall, hit a picture and it crashed on to the floor.

If the hostility over the assets of their deceased sister were not enough, there was also a divergence of opinion over the rights of two nephews to inherit. Those nephews were the living children of another deceased sister. The law allowed those nephews to step into the shoes of their deceased mother. However, the surviving sisters, who were participating in the turmoil in that boardroom, had received an inaccurate legal opinion to the effect that the nephews had no status in the estate, particularly because those nephews had been estranged from the family. As it turns out, this opinion did not come from a lawyer, but rather from a travel agent who happened to be the neighbor of one of the sisters. The opinion of the travel agent was of course very comforting to the sisters. It was in their own interests that the estate not be diluted by the further participation of these nephews. When we tried to explain that the law gave these nephews an interest in the estate because the deceased sister died without a Will, the hostility of the surviving sisters was turned toward us, making them even more difficult to reason with. What all of the individuals in that boardroom forgot, was that while they were bickering and disputing and attacking each other:

- the fact was that the estate itself had no representation;

- the estate was completely frozen;

- there were, in all likelihood, undiscovered assets;

- there were existing assets which had to be protected, an example of which was the deceased sister's empty house and her car in the driveway. Someone had to maintain insurance coverage on these valuable assets.

During the multiple confrontations described above, the estate was not yet represented by anyone who had enforceable rights and the group was heading in the direction of hiring various lawyers to represent various interests. The meeting broke up without any hope of progress. The entire group of siblings ended the meeting rather unceremoniously. Through the window we could see them arguing in the parking lot after they left.

The unfortunate situation that we have just described leads us to make the following observation: We would say that if their deceased sister could have seen her family in tatters, she would have done anything to turn back the clock and make a Will to avoid this family disaster.

SUGGESTED PLANNING STRATEGIES– NARROWING THE FOCUS

We have to realize, and it goes without saying, that there are some problems that even the best planning cannot resolve. Where old wounds exist, such as pre-existing animosities, estrangement of children, parents or siblings, separation, divorce and conflicts between stepchildren and stepparents, it is rather idealistic to suggest that proper planning will serve to resolve matters of this nature. However, overall and looking at the vast majority of situations, what we would say is that for most families, proper planning will be a major component in holding the family members together.

Now that we have a grasp on the importance of planning from a general point of view, let us narrow our focus and examine some important planning strategies which deserve special attention. We will consider strategies relating to the following twelve matters:

- Durable Powers of Attorney for Property and Health;
- Your Will: appointment of executors;
- Your Will: when you wish to exclude a child;
- Your Will: the use of trusts;
- Your Will: the caregiving child;

- Your Will: avoiding inadvertent inequality;
- Dealing with your family home;
- Dealing with your family business;
- Living separate and apart;
- Second marriage planning;
- Making changes to your Will;
- Life insurance.

DURABLE POWERS OF ATTORNEY FOR PROPERTY AND HEALTH

When you are thinking of having your lawyer prepare a Durable Power of Attorney for Property it will be helpful for you to think of the following questions. If you have two children, are you going to appoint both children so they must act together, or will you allow one of the two children to act independently of the other? If you appoint three or more children, will you require unanimity of all of those children, or will your appointment allow a majority of those children to make a decision? These are some appointment options available to you, and before you decide, you have to really know your own family situation. Can your children easily work together? Do they all live in the same State? If you have one child who lives in your State and one child who lives outside of your State, will you be creating an inconvenience if your Power of Attorney requires both children to act together? What do your children think? If you are putting a majority clause in your document, will two strong children overpower a weak one? Certainly, you should seek professional help on this very important decision. If you choose wrongly, you could create dissension among your children. In considering a Durable Power of Attorney for Property, never lose sight of the importance of appointing someone you trust. The appointment of one or more persons who are anything short of trustworthy can lead to potential abuse.

A few final words on this point: if you have only one child, you may wish to consider appointing a backup attorney in the event that your child dies before you do, or becomes unable or unwilling to act on your behalf. In considering appointing your child, you should be satisfied that the child has the maturity, the willingness and the ability to carry out the functions that will be required. This applies as well to any backup attorneys whom you are contemplating. If you have no children, or if any of the children you have cannot meet these requirements, you may think about appointing a trusted niece or nephew, or a trusted friend or even a trusted financial institution. These same appointment considerations will apply to your Durable Power of Attorney for Health Care.

Some jurisdictions allow for the creation of a Power of Attorney for Property which is sometimes referred to as a "springing" Power of Attorney. This type of Power of Attorney is one which is created so that it will not take effect until a certain event specified in the document takes place. Quite commonly, the event which is contemplated consists of a doctor certifying that you have lost your mental capacity. In other words, until that particular event arises, a springing Power of Attorney simply cannot yet be used. Some people take comfort from a springing Power of Attorney because they realize that it cannot be used until the triggering event takes place. While this may be of comfort to those who have some element of mistrust in the person they have appointed, there are difficulties with this position which deserve some explanation.

Suppose that you sign a springing Power of Attorney which specifically provides that the attorney appointed in the document will have power to act for you when one doctor certifies that you have become mentally incapable. Suppose, however, that you are suffering from a debilitating physical ailment such as Parkinson's disease or Multiple Sclerosis. You could be unable to go to the bank to sign your name and you could be unable to carry on day to day business and as a result you may require someone to carry out these functions for you. However, when the attorney you appointed presents your springing Power of Attorney to the bank, the bank will require evidence that you were certified by a doctor to be mentally incapable strictly in accordance with the wording of the springing Power of Attorney. Here is the problem that emanates from the above situation: no doctor will certify you to be mentally incapable because Parkinson's disease and Multiple Sclerosis are physical ailments, not mental ailments. As a result, your attorney will have no power to act for you even though you require his or her help. Now you can see some possible difficulties with the wording contained in a springing Power of Attorney. The point is, that until the event specified in the springing Power of Attorney actually takes place, the attorney simply cannot act.

On the other hand, those who have full trust in their appointees can have their lawyers draft a Durable Power of Attorney for Property which sidesteps all of the triggering language, so that it is fully effective as soon as this type of Durable Power of Attorney for Property is given to the trusted appointee. Since there is no triggering language in the document, it will be effective without the necessity to resort to any doctor certification. It follows as a matter of logic that this type of Durable Power of Attorney for Property will be effective in circumstances of both physical and mental incapacity.

Regardless of which form of Power of Attorney you create, before you name anyone on it, you should have a full and frank discussion with the person you are about to name. In that discussion, you might find, somewhat to your surprise, that the one whom you thought would want to act as your attorney, may express a wish not to do so because of concerns for his or her own inconvenience. In situations of this nature, silence is not necessarily golden. You should be communicating with the person you trust, unless there is a very good reason not to.

The above considerations bring us to the question as to who should be appointed. To begin with, it should be remembered that the word "attorney" in the context of Durable Power of Attorney does not mean your lawyer. Attorney is the word used to designate the person who represents you.

Typically, in a first marriage situation, each of the spouses will appoint the other, assuming that each of the spouses is willing and capable of carrying out this type of function. When a Durable Power of Attorney is being created, typically the parties will consider appointing one or more capable children to act as backup attorneys. Of course, if there are no such children, spouses may then cast their eyes toward a trusted sibling. No one is compelled in law to appoint a spouse or a child or a sibling. However, the most likely candidates for such appointment fall within these relationships as a rule.

When it comes to a second or subsequent marriage, the spouses may feel more comfortable appointing their respective children from each of their first marriages as attorneys. Typically, same sex or common law partners will tend to appoint each other because of their close relationship. In considering the consequences of separation or divorce, you should seek some advice as to whether the law in your State will allow the Power of Attorney you created during marriage to survive your separation or divorce. By receiving the appropriate advice, you will be made aware as to any urgent necessity to revoke the Powers of Attorney that you had given to the spouse from whom you are now about to be separated or divorced. Our reference to urgency comes from our concern that the person whom you initially appointed, and from you are now separated or divorced, may still have access to your bank accounts and other assets, if the Power of Attorney continues unrevoked.

Before leaving the subject of naming parties, there is one more consideration to deal with. Suppose you have three children, all of whom are going to be excellent candidates to be named on a Durable Power of Attorney for Property. However, of the three children, one may require a few more years before he or she is mature enough to be named. In such a case, you must periodically review your documentation so that you will know when to make the appropriate amendments in order that the capable young person becomes one of your trusted representatives. Take advantage of your opportunities to review and revise your documentation because if you become incapacitated at a later date, your incapacity will prevent you from being able to make any further changes to your documentation.

On a parallel to the Durable Power of Attorney for Property, we can talk about strategies associated with the Durable Power of Attorney for Health Care and Living Will.

Firstly, avoid putting these documents in a safety deposit box  because they are going to be required in medical circumstances. If a medical crisis arises after banking hours, the documentation will not be accessible from a safety deposit box. Furthermore, if you are living on your own, you should seriously consider putting a written location note on the door of your refrigerator, so that emergency personnel who enter your home in the event of an emergency will know where to find your Power of Attorney documentation and who you have appointed on the document, as your representative. As well, it would be a good idea to include your medical history with the document, so that allergies, previous operations, blood type, etc. will be available to emergency personnel who may have to look after you. Some people also carry locator cards in their wallets, which will point people to the location of the Power of Attorney.

The representative you choose for this Power of Attorney can certainly be the same as the representative you choose for your Durable Power of Attorney for Property. However, we are not speaking about a legal matter but a practical matter here. There may be reasons why the child who is going to work out so well as your financial representative may not be the one who works out so well as your representative for medical and personal care purposes. You are going to have to exercise wisdom in making these choices. Bearing in mind that the purpose of this particular Power of Attorney is to make decisions governing your medical and personal care situation, you will want the person you appoint to live close enough so that he or she can get to you in short order. Physical location is important here. Remember that he or she will have to deal with doctors, nurses and other medical personnel. You should also ensure that the person or persons you are appointing have a grasp of your medical history. You should also indicate where your medical records are kept.

Be absolutely sure that your documents are up to date. You will want to know whether they are effective and will survive serious changes in your life, such as a move to another State or a change in the law of your State. As an adult child, you should tell your own parents to review their documents on a regular basis. It may have made sense a number of years ago for your father to have appointed his brother, but today that appointment may have little practical benefit if your father's brother is very elderly or if there is hostility between your father and his brother. It would be especially frustrating for your father's brother to take precedence over you if you were perfectly capable and had a loving relationship with your father.

YOUR WILL: APPOINTMENT OF EXECUTORS

If you are considering appointing three or more children as your executors, consider inserting a majority clause in your Will. Such a clause will allow the decision of the majority of your executors to bind your estate and thereby avoid a deadlock among them. However, a majority clause may not be applicable in all situations. In some families, a majority clause might enable two of your executors to consistently outvote the third. If the prospect of this pattern of voting is of concern to you, a majority clause may not be the ideal solution in such a particular situation. As an alternative, you might consider providing in your Will for a different form of decision making: all decisions would have to be unanimous. Unanimity will certainly solve the concern to which we have just made reference. Of course, the downside of the unanimous decision format is that in the absence of unanimity, your executors may be forced to go to court to resolve any serious impasse. As long as one executor is withholding consent, the estate will be deadlocked. We can only suggest that before making a decision on this point, you have to know your own family. Do not turn your back on this most important issue.

We cannot overemphasize how important it is to periodically review the appointment of your executors in your Will. If you appointed your brother as executor twenty years ago, the appointment certainly could have made sense at that time. However, the appointment may be sadly out of date today if your brother is elderly, distant from your children, either by way of geographical distance, or, emotionally, by way of a cool relationship with them. By keeping your brother as executor in these circumstances, you may be frustrating your mature and loyal children, all of whom are quite ready, willing and able to take on the task themselves. A more dramatic example of this type of problem consists of a Will appointing your former accountant as executor. You could be burdening your children, as beneficiaries under your Will, with a cool and distant executor, who is well aware of his rights to compensation from your estate, not only as executor, but also as a professional. Your children may find such an appointment to be most unwelcome. They may in the end, after your death, be struggling with this situation, attempting to persuade that professional to abandon the appointment in circumstances where the professional may be quite unwilling to abandon it without compensation.

It is perfectly acceptable and very common to name someone as both executor and beneficiary under your Will. Certainly, there is no conflict between these positions. By way of a reminder, it is advisable to name a backup executor in your Will wherever possible, whether that backup executor is a beneficiary or not. Problems will arise where you have failed to name a backup executor and your primary executor is for some reason no longer willing or able to serve.

Before leaving this subject, one final point: If you choose as your executor, someone who resides outside of the country, such executor may be compelled to post security in court before carrying on the administration of your estate. You should be obtaining legal advice from your lawyer on this point before designating anyone who resides outside of the country as executor.

YOUR WILL: WHEN YOU WISH
TO EXCLUDE A CHILD

If, after all considerations, you are absolutely determined that one of your adult children is to be excluded from benefiting from your estate, we would recommend some protective measures to be taken, as a bare minimum, in addition to taking advice from your legal representative. At the very least, you should be writing a letter outside of your Will stating your reasoning for excluding that particular child. The letter might state, for example, that you have not seen the child for over twenty years, or that the child has unequivocally abandoned the family, or perhaps that the child has become extremely wealthy and that it is in the best interests of his or her siblings that you direct your estate to those of your children who really need the money. In this latter situation, of course, it would be wise to provide one or more small mementos taken from your personal possessions, which would have sentimental significance to that particular child, in order to minimize any negative feelings. One of the benefits of such a letter, from the point of the view of the child who was cut out, will be that he or she will see your reasoning for excluding him or her. Furthermore, this same letter will lessen the burden on his or her siblings because everyone will know what your reasoning was and the siblings will be less likely to feel guilty in benefiting from the exclusion of the child to which we have just made reference. Finally, if ever the matter of your intention was contested, the letter would constitute some evidence of your intentions, notwithstanding that the letter itself cannot be interpreted as a Will.

In addition to such an explanatory letter, you would also be wise to obtain a letter from your doctor to show that at the time you made your Will, you had sufficient mental capacity to do so. The letter from

your doctor will be of immense help to
those of your children whom you intend
to benefit because it will assist them if and
when the child who was cut out launches
an attack on your Will. In choosing the

doctor, of course, you must exercise common sense. It should be a
doctor who has sufficient familiarity with your mental capacity to
withstand cross-examination in court if the matter became hotly contested. Finally, in considering a situation of this nature where your
capacity may be intact, but you have experienced declining health, and
perhaps some minor impairment to your memory, it would be prudent to upgrade the type of letter we are describing so that it is provided by a medical practitioner who specializes in the recognition of
cognitive ability and mental capacity. You should recognize that in the
interval of time between the date that you make your Will and the
time that you pass away, it is possible that you may experience further
impairment to your mental capacity, and after you are gone there may
be allegations made by those who wish to attack your Will bringing
into focus, a serious impairment to your cognitive abilities. The value
of a letter of this nature would be to bring back into focus, the fact that
your cognitive abilities may have declined significantly in your later
years, but that your cognitive abilities certainly were intact at the time
that you made your Will.

One further thought with respect to enhancing the defense of your
Will: In circumstances where an excluded child intends to launch an
attack on your Will, your estate's defense will be significantly
enhanced if the Will were to be prepared by a lawyer as opposed to
being a homemade Will. A lawyer drawn Will should be much easier
to defend in such circumstances.

Despite all of the above comments, we would nevertheless urge extreme caution before excluding a child from your estate. The cause of your feelings may be temporary, and you may have chosen to act impulsively in taking this step. Alternatively, your motivation might have come from something which was said or done by the child which took you by surprise and to which you reacted. One of the most important considerations here is to realize that down the road you may choose to re-insert that child in your Will. It would be tragic if, as a result of incapacity or death, you were unable to revise your Will to once again include that child. You can only imagine how hurt and upset that child would be, if, having resolved all matters with you, he or she was still excluded from your estate. The resulting animosity of that child, over time, could ultimately reflect itself in court proceedings and also in the relationship which that child has with his or her siblings.

Given your determination to effect this exclusion, we will draw on a recurring theme of this book, to the effect that you should be communicating your feelings to those whom you believe will survive you. Accordingly, if you are resolved and determined to take the step of excluding such a child, it might be advisable for you to take one further step before making that final decision. That further step would be to discuss with the children who will inherit, your feelings about excluding their sibling. To your surprise, the children who are to inherit may prefer to take a little less from your estate in order to maintain their relationship with the child whom you are considering excluding. They may wish you to reconsider in order to lift the burden of stress and confrontation from them. They may prefer that, to at least some extent, you include their sibling, so that after you are gone, they can enjoy a warm relationship which might otherwise be denied them.

There is yet another method of approaching an unequal or disproportionate distribution of your estate, without excluding a child from your Will. You may consider preparing your Will so that all of your children take equally, including the child whom you feel is not as deserving as his or her brothers and sisters. However, you might consider speaking to your lawyer about the steps which you can take in order to configure your estate in a manner that best fulfills your wishes, given the above circumstances. In describing the steps which are available to you, we would utilize the term "favored children" to describe those children who are to take the greatest benefit and we will utilize the term "the target child" to describe the one who would have been cut out of your Will if you were unaware of these strategies. The steps available to you to accomplish your purposes may include the following:

- You would provide outright gifts during your lifetime to the favored children, but not the target child;
- You would name the favored children as beneficiaries on life insurance policies, but not the target child;
- You would hold property jointly with right of survivorship between yourself and the favored children, but would not name the target child.

Of course there are tax consequences, creditor and marital considerations involved in these strategies, which you should discuss with your accountant and your lawyer. However, what you will accomplish through utilizing these strategies will be to minimize the risk of an attack on your Will because your Will, in these circumstances, would be leaving the rest of your estate equally to all of your children.

YOUR WILL: THE USE OF TRUSTS

Previously in this book, we have discussed the difference between an outright gift and a gift held in trust. With this information in mind, we can now examine a number of strategies available to you by using trusts within your Will. To illustrate clearly how a trust can be utilized in this fashion, let us take a look at a few examples. It should be borne in mind that the first of these examples will not only illustrate this point, but will also show you a viable and practical alternative to excluding a child from your Will, in certain circumstances.

Suppose you have two children, one of whom has a severe addiction problem and certainly cannot handle money. You may consider excluding that child from your Will because you feel that any gift to that child would be a total waste. Money would be squandered. On the other hand, cutting out the child could create very bad feelings and this exclusion could work severe hardship on that child which, taken to the extreme, might have the effect of driving that child, in almost the worst of circumstances, to poverty and public shelter. There is a middle ground whereby you can protect the child with the addiction problem and ensure that he is not impoverished and whereby you can protect your assets at the same time, and ensure that they are not squandered by the addicted child. This is where the trust in your Will can come in. You could include the child with the addiction problem by, for example, setting aside a sum of money in a trust for him, for his lifetime. The trustee you name in your Will to look after that money would manage and invest it and also have the right to pay out income to that child for the rest of his life. At the same time, that child would never be able to squander the capital because only the trustee would have access to it. Furthermore, at the time you are setting up the trust, you may wish to include among the other powers involved in the trust, a power of invasion or encroachment over the capital. By doing so, you would be addressing certain situations which might arise in the life of that child. Perhaps his income, combined with the income of the trust, will be insufficient to cover a medical emergency or to cover some other significant requirement in his life. The rights of invasion of capital of which we are speaking would allow your trustee to encroach upon or invade the capital of the trust to the extent necessary to make the money available to cover such requirement.

The trust should also be drafted to provide that when the child with the addiction passes away, whatever is left unused out of the assets contained in the trust, will be inherited by another beneficiary of your choosing. It should also be borne in mind that the designation of your trustee is critically important. You may be fortunate enough to have a trustworthy family member, consisting of a sibling or another child, who would be willing and able to carry out this function. You have to be aware that although it is an honor to be named in such a capacity, the position carries with it significant burdens of time and possibly stressful judgment calls. These considerations would be of particular concern in the event that you appointed one child as trustee to look after money set aside for the benefit of his or her sibling. Usually, an alternative would be to appoint a neutral trustee, such as a financial institution.

There are, of course, other situations where the use of a trust becomes invaluable. The next example that comes to mind involves the preservation of the inheritance of your children so that their money becomes available to them at a point in time when they have become mature enough to handle it. To accomplish this, you could instruct your lawyer to prepare a trust in your Will which would postpone your child's inheritance until that child reaches the age of twenty-five or, in a more conservative example, the age of thirty.

Yet another option would be to provide for a part of the gift to be paid out at the age of twenty-one, another part at the age of twenty-five, another part at the age of thirty, and the balance at the age of thirty-five. The examples, of course, can vary in accordance with the required circumstances. In addition, you might want to consider instructing your lawyer to include a right of invasion or encroachment upon the capital of that trust by the trustee, so that the trustee can exercise his or her discretion for the purpose of utilizing some of the income or capital contained in the trust, in order to address certain requirements of your children. In discussing such requirements, we would normally consider education, medical needs, expenses necessary to maintain a certain lifestyle and other similar matters. We must emphasize that in creating rights of invasion or encroachment, you are treading upon an area which will require the expertise of a lawyer. If the encroachment rights are not drafted widely enough, your trustees may run into a problem in attempting to assist your children. A good example to illustrate a limitation of this nature would be a right of encroachment or invasion of capital for the sole purpose of enabling your trustees to pay for post-secondary education of your children. Bear in mind that we are discussing a situation where the child in question would be, for example, twenty years old and the postponement of the gift to that child would provide the capital of the trust to him or to her at the age of twenty-five. It is in that interim period that the illustration becomes dramatic. Remember that we are discussing wording inserted in a trust which enables the trustee to encroach upon capital for the sole purpose of paying for the post-secondary education of your child. What if that child requires special medical care that is not covered by a medical plan, or requires a car for his or her job? The trustee will not be able to encroach upon the monies of the trust to accomplish these purposes because the wording of the trust was too narrow to permit such an encroachment. To further reinforce the complexity of this area, in some jurisdictions, depending upon where you live, your lawyer may have to consider providing for a situation where your child does not live to reach the age specified in the trust. Your lawyer may have to provide for what is known as a gift over to benefit a different beneficiary in such circumstances. Furthermore, your lawyer may have to address issues relating to income which is accumulating during this period.

You might be tempted to avoid all of these issues, and take comfort in the presumption that by the time you pass away, your children will be in their forties or fifties. The difficulty with this form of reasoning is that it ignores the true risks of life. If indeed you happen to pass away leaving one or more young children, in circumstances where you have prepared your Will without confronting all of the issues we have just described, your children will inherit as soon as they reach the age of majority. In many States, the age of majority is eighteen. Can you imagine the peer pressure imposed upon a child who inherits $500,000.00 at that age? Unless the child is unusually mature, there is a substantial risk that the money will be squandered.

In the context of avoiding family fights, let us now illustrate how the squandering of such money can put one sibling at the throat of another. Imagine, taking our story further, that your daughter, within a couple of years of her inheritance, has managed to dissipate her entire fortune, perhaps living a life of luxury or investing the money very unwisely. Meanwhile, your conservative son not only has the initial investment intact, but has managed to build it up even higher.

There is every likelihood that your daughter may ask your son for assistance. This could create tension between your son and your daughter if your son happens to be married to a woman who wishes your son to resist the request of your daughter. We might summarize all of this as follows: by failing to prepare your Will with appropriate trust provisions you have:

- allowed your daughter to squander her portion of the estate; and
- put your son under pressure from both his wife and his sister, whereby he can only satisfy one of them at the expense of his relationship with the other.

YOUR WILL: THE CAREGIVING CHILD

We often see instances of individuals who have aging parents to care for, in addition to their own young children. All too often, such individuals are forced to restrict or even give up their education and their careers in order to accommodate the needs of their aging parents. Such needs are likely to involve shopping trips, appointments with doctors and dentists, opticians and other health care providers. Included as part of the appointment process are long periods of waiting room time. These needs can escalate even to the point of the child having to become a full time caregiver to the parent in his or her own home. All of this is being specified so that the following comments can be put in proper perspective. In a situation where the aging parent has a number of children, it is more than likely that the caregiving obligations will fall on the shoulders of one or perhaps two of those children, but not on the shoulders of all of them. In such situations, it is most important not to trivialize the burdens which fall upon those of the children who happen to carry out the caregiving function.

Accordingly, a delicate question arises on the subject of proper monetary and financial treatment of a caregiving child in such circumstances. It is very easy to make an error which will result in conflict among your children. If you are perceived to have overly favored or benefited the caregiving child, his or her siblings may form the impression that the caregiver was simply a favored child. On the other hand, if one prepares an estate ignoring the distinction between the caregiving child and the non-caregiving children, it is likely that the child who devoted himself or herself to such caregiving will feel exploited, unappreciated and embittered. Such feelings have a way of turning into animosity over time. You may have inadvertently created a festering bitterness within the caregiving child that will express itself in his or her relationship with your other children. As you can see, we are faced here with somewhat of a small margin of error. How does one walk the tightrope without erring on one side or the other?

To begin with, you have to remember that your Will is not the only method of conferring a benefit. Also, no one can confer an exact monetary value upon the heartfelt contribution of a caregiving child. With this in mind, you may consider giving one or more gifts of money or personal items to the child during your life, accompanied by a letter expressing your reasons for doing this, and indicating that the gifts are a gesture of appreciation for the special efforts of that child in looking after you. Alternatively, you may choose to name that child as the beneficiary on a policy of insurance which you might otherwise have made payable to your estate. This, too, should be dealt with

in a personal letter or memorandum from you expressing why you have named that particular child in that particular policy of insurance. Such a letter of explanation should go very far in explaining to the non-caregiving children, the importance that you have attached to the efforts of the caregiving child. The letter should be prepared with the following thought in mind: Its purpose is to go as far as possible in explaining to the non-caregiving children that the benefit being conferred upon their caregiving sibling is consistent with the time, effort and sacrifice of the caregiving child and should therefore never be looked upon as being disproportionate or excessive in any manner.

A further alternative to the gift during your lifetime or the naming of the child in a policy of insurance is the conferring of an extra benefit to the caregiving child in your Will. In considering this extra benefit, you must be reasonable. If, for example, you were to give everything to the caregiving child, to the exclusion of your other children, it is almost certain that this sort of a gift would be looked upon as unreasonable and in all likelihood there would be conflict among your children after you passed away. In determining what is reasonable, you will have to consider the circumstances of your own particular situation and it would be very wise for you to discuss this matter with the lawyer who is preparing your Will. For example, it would appear from a general standpoint that equality among all of your children, subject to a special monetary gift in favor of the caregiving child, would be looked upon as a much softer approach than an uneven split among the children which favors the caregiving child. You would be wise to consider discussing with your lawyer, the feasibility of utilizing wording in your Will which explains, right in your Will, the reason for giving that special monetary gift to your caregiving child. An example would be

"To my son Robert, I leave the sum of $25,000.00 in gratitude for his years of personal sacrifice in looking after me." If you decide to confer a special benefit upon your caregiving child in your Will, it is always advisable to prepare a separate letter which sets out your reasons for conferring that benefit, even though it may be repeating the reasoning already stated in your Will. Such a letter can only help your caregiving child in addressing any form of discontent which his or her siblings may express, after you pass away. One last, very important point before we leave this particular subject: Before conferring a special benefit on your caregiving child, you may wish to have a discussion with him or with her as to whether that child wishes such a benefit in the first place. To your surprise, the caregiving child may prefer not to have the special benefit, in order to avoid any confrontation with his or her siblings. He or she will certainly appreciate that you raised the subject. You may appreciate the fact that your child has been looking after you out of love, and not for money.

YOUR WILL: AVOIDING INADVERTENT INEQUALITY

Let us assume that your intention is to treat all of your children equally. As good as your intentions are, it is always possible that you may be overlooking something which can, in the end, after you pass away, tear your family apart. Such a situation is illustrated by what we term inadvertent inequality. The term describes a situation where you certainly intend to create equality among your children, but in fact, it is your poor planning or your oversights or your erroneous assumptions which lead your estate to the very inequality you intended to avoid. That having been said, let us now examine some illustrations which will show how inadvertent inequality can occur.

Suppose you have three children, one of whom may require money for a university education. Your other children are working and have no desire for a university education. Of course, if all of your children had expressed a wish and had the ability to go to university, you would have been more than happy to spend thousands of dollars for a university education for each and every one of them. However, in this particular situation, life did not work out that way. In the example at hand, you may well be spending tens of thousands of dollars on the one child's university education. All the while, your other children never comment on the situation, but this does not necessarily disclose to you what their true feelings are. Many years later, when it comes time to do your Will planning, the passage of time may have removed from your mind, the fact that you spent tens of thousands of dollars on one of your children, without spending any comparable sums on the others. Although you may have forgotten about this discrepancy, you can almost rest assured that those of your children who did not receive the university money have not forgotten the fact that many years ago, you benefited their sibling, and rather substantially, at that.

If, under these circumstances, you then plan your Will with a view to leaving everything you own equally among all of your children, you may, by your failure to give proper consideration to the benefits which we have just discussed, be creating grounds for jealousy or hurt feelings in the minds and emotions of those children who never did get the type of benefit that was bestowed upon the child who went to university. In order to minimize the type of problem which could result from this example of inadvertent inequality, you might consider leaving a sum of money in your Will to those of your children who did not receive money for a university education. With this balancing pattern of gifts in your Will, you can then divide your estate equally among your children with a clear mind. You will recall the benefits of leaving a letter with your Will, which explains your reasoning for leaving a particular gift. This is the very type of situation where it would be appropriate to prepare and leave a letter of this kind.

Another alternative might be to consider, during your lifetime, giving to those other children, gifts of money equal to the gift that you gave to the child who received the university education. Gifts of this nature might be tailored to helping them pay down their mortgage or some similar matter. Of course, to the extent that there are any tax implications, you should speak to your lawyer in order to obtain the proper advice.

Let us now turn to another example of a situation where you once again create inadvertent inequality. This example is confined to gifts contained in your Will. Suppose that in your Will you decide to give a personal item of considerable value to one of your children, such as a stamp collection or a hockey card collection. At the time of making your Will, you have a perception of the value of that particular gift and you may even take the trouble to obtain an appraisal. Based upon your perceived value of that gift, you then attempt to equalize that gift by providing a money gift to your other child or your other children of a value equivalent to the value that you have affixed to the gift of the collection we just referred to. However, over time, the value of that particular collection might fluctuate, rather significantly. A failure to review and consequently revise your Will could lead to the following form of inadvertent inequality: imagine that the value that you gave to the collection at the time that you made your Will was $10,000.00, and the balancing gifts to your other children, who did not receive the collection, were each in the sum of $10,000.00, so that you came away from the exercise with full equivalence. However, by the time of your death, the value of that collection has risen from $10,000.00 to $100,000.00, thereby destroying the equality that you tried so hard to accomplish in your Will. As a result, once again, the children who received the $10,000.00 gifts might possibility look with some degree of envy at their sibling who received the $100,000.00 collection. Before leaving this subject, it is also possible that the reverse situation could take place. It is entirely possible that the collection could have depreciated in value by the time of your death, reversing the feelings that we have just described. In order to minimize this type of a problem it is very important to continue to review your Will on a regular basis.

DEALING WITH YOUR FAMILY HOME

For most of us, our family home is one of our most valuable assets. In planning your Will, there are a number of issues to consider which relate to this most valuable asset. The purpose of this commentary is not to give an exhaustive list of all of the issues that can arise in dealing with the family home, but we do feel that it is important to offer a sampling of some of the more important issues that are often overlooked, but which are likely to arise. Oversights with respect to these issues can lead to family friction after your death.

The first issue to be addressed would be the situation where you have three children, two of whom have their own homes and one of whom lives at home with you. Question: Do you leave the home to the child who lives there with you or do you leave the home in your Will to be divided equally among those children who survive you? A second issue arises here because if you decide to leave that home to the child who lives there with you, do you then compensate his or her siblings with a gift of money or another asset? Think of this issue in light of the discussion regarding inadvertent inequality. Assuming that you wish to leave your home equally to all of your children, what happens to the child who was living in the home? Will that child have enough in the way of assets to buy out his or her siblings? If he or she does not have enough to buy them out, will the estate decide to sell that home in the marketplace and split the money up among the children? Of course, if that happens, the child who had been living in the house loses possession of it and has to find another place to live.

Suppose, after great thought, you decide that you are going to leave your home to the one child who had been living there. What do you do about the contents of that home? Will all of the furniture and personal effects go to that one child along with the home or will the furniture and personal effects be divided among all of your children? If you decide to divide the contents among the three children, friction could easily develop when the other children show up to remove their share of the furniture and personal effects from the home. This is capable of creating hostility among your children because of the emotional nature of personal effects. On the other hand, if you decide that the child who inherits the house will also inherit all of its contents, you should make sure that the language in your Will on this point is very explicit. A gift of the house does not necessarily mean a gift of the contents. Your Will should clearly state that the child who inherits the house will also receive the contents, if that is what you intend to happen. Give great thought to

personal effects because of the nostalgia and personal attachment which your children might feel for these items. If you are going to leave all of the personal effects in your home to one child, bear in mind that those of your children who do not receive any of your personal effects which were contained in your home, are likely to feel deprived. We can only urge you to be very sensitive to the types of emotions involved when you are dealing with personal effects in the home.

Let us now consider the matter of your family home, mortgaged, and left to someone in your Will. Assuming that your estate plan does not go to the point of building in mortgage insurance, you must deal with the question of who is going to carry the burden of that mortgage. Will it be the child who inherits the home or your estate? If it is your intention that your estate pay the mortgage, you have to consider how all of your other children, the ones who did not receive the home in your Will, are going to feel about your estate having to make monthly mortgage payments on a home in which they have no interest. Such payments will reduce their share. This is a personal matter, of course, but it should be dealt with specifically in your discussions with your lawyer.

This leads us to a commentary on those who try to deal with the subject matter of their home in a homemade Will. Many who create homemade Wills not only ignore the above issues, but also fail to consider what happens if, after completing their Will, they happen to sell the family home and move into another one. They may inadvertently leave open the question as to whether the replacement home is to be treated in the same way as the home referred to in the homemade Will. Generally speaking, a professionally prepared Will in all likelihood will cover all of these situations because the lawyer is likely to raise the issues with you before the Will is drafted.

Yet another problem can arise where the person who is trying to create his estate plan fails to grasp the difference between two kinds of co-ownership of the family home. In one type of co-ownership, there is a deed to the parties as joint tenants with right of survivorship. In order to illustrate the meaning of joint tenancy, we will use the following example. Imagine that you are widowed and that you have three children. Imagine further that you are holding the property together with one son and each of you is a joint tenant. If you die, your son automatically becomes owner of that particular property, by operation of law, because that is how joint tenancy works in law, no matter what your Will may say. To delve yet further into that point, if your Will gave the property equally to your three children, the joint tenancy would override that provision in your Will on the grounds that you cannot give in a Will what you do not own, and you do not own that property at the date of your death because of the joint tenancy. Now you can begin to realize what serious repercussions can develop from a failure to grasp the difference between joint tenancy and other types of co-ownership. Typically, one other type of co-ownership is known in law as tenants in common. The definition of tenants in common when it comes to the ownership of real estate, is essentially the same as the concept of partnership. When one of the tenants in common passes away, his or her share in the property will pass through his or her Will to his or her estate, leaving intact, the other half of the property which the other owner will continue to own.

There is one further consideration which we would like to bring forth on the subject of joint ownership. Whether you have one child or three, the fact is that when you name any child to be a joint owner with you, you have to realize that you are effectively giving a share of the ownership of that property to that child during the time that you and your child or children are alive. There are certain facts of life which then arise. You must realize that there are a number of situations which will expose the share in the house that you have deeded to any child or children, examples of which are as follows:

- what if your child or children have creditors, either governmental or business creditors?

- what if your child or children may be subject to bankruptcy or insolvency problems?

- what if your child or children have signed a serious financial guarantee which may go into default, the consequences of which may create financial adversity?

- what if your child or children are undergoing actual or potential marital problems?

You must realize that in all of the above situations, you have actually deeded a share in your home to someone who is at risk. The consequence of that risk puts your home itself into jeopardy, even though you may still own part of it.

You should also seek some tax advice before a naming a child or children as co-owners on a family home. There may be some adverse tax consequences to consider if you choose to take such steps. The risks to which we have just made reference are not confined to joint tenancy situations. They are common to any form of co-ownership of the family home.

DEALING WITH YOUR FAMILY BUSINESS

When we consider the subject matter of the family business, we are raising a subject which can be quite complex. As you may appreciate, entire books are written on the subject matter of succession planning for a family business. All we intend to do here is to raise a few issues which should be borne in mind. In

John Smith Manufacturing Inc.

addressing these issues, we would point out that there are three ways, generally, in which a family business can be operated. In its simplest version, the family business can be run as a sole proprietorship, where the person making the Will is the only owner of the business. Another manner of operating the business consists of a partnership of two or more individuals. The third form of operating a business consists of corporate ownership of the business, with shares in the corporation being held at least in part by the person making the Will. In considering succession planning, you should be made aware that in a partnership situation or in a corporate situation where there is more than one shareholder, there is likely to be a partnership agreement or a shareholder agreement which contains provisions which in some manner restrict the ability of any of the partners or any of the co-shareholders to leave their interests to beneficiaries under a Will. For the purposes of this particular discussion, we will assume that the business is run as a corporation and that you own all of the shares in that corporation.

Assuming, then, as we have above, that your business is run as a corporation and that you own all of its shares, the professional advice which is in all likelihood available to you, will be to the effect that among other options, you have the ability to transfer the shares in your corporation, either during your life or after your death. In the particular discussion which is about to follow, we will concentrate on the method of transferring the shares in your corporation after your death.

The fundamental question revolves around who is going to inherit the business from you. If you are survived by a spouse and children, the primary consideration must be, who among them has the capability and the desire to operate this business after you pass away. The range of possibilities, of course, is on the one extreme, that every one of them is able and willing, and on the other extreme, that none of them are either able or willing. If in any version of the answer, your spouse is both willing and able to operate the business, your focus might then be to obtain the appropriate tax advice to determine whether there exists a tax-free method of transferring your interests from yourself to your spouse. In many jurisdictions, there may be a facility of this nature which exists from spouse to spouse, but which would not exist in a transfer from parent to child.

We then come to the next consideration, assuming that you have supportive tax advice, which is whether those who inherit the business from you can get along with each other as owners and operators. What brings this question to mind is the image of a surviving spouse inheriting the business along with your children. You cannot assume that their interests and their future visions will be compatible, one with the other. For example, your spouse may not hold the view that he or she should work day and night to expand the business, contrary to the philosophy of some of your children who may wish to expend considerable energy and undertake considerable risk with a view to preparing for expansion and hopefully wealth in their later years. Assuming that some or all of these concerns are applicable, you can readily see that your good intentions to divide your business equally, can create hostility among those you love.

Another scenario might be where one of several children actively participates in the business, but the others do not. Your leaning will probably be to leave the business to the child who built it up with you. However, what do you do to compensate his or her siblings? It is almost a certainty that you will not spread your business interests equally among all of the children so that you can achieve equality among them. To do so will in all likelihood create very hard feelings within the mind of the child who worked so hard to build the business up. He would see his siblings benefiting from his own efforts and his own sacrifices. However, we are phrasing this situation as almost a certainty. There is always a remote possibility that in certain circumstances the person planning his or her estate may in fact wish that all of the children for some reason take the business together. In this context, there is also the remote possibility that in such circumstances, the child who worked so hard to build up the business may in fact have no objection to his or her siblings joining the company. However, on balance, the likelihood of such situations arising is extremely remote, human nature being what it is.

That leads us to the next logical question, which is equalization among all of your children by compensating the ones who do not get the business, with a non-business asset. Assuming, to begin with, that the configuration of your estate is such that there indeed are other assets with which to compensate the children who are not inheriting the business, then your logical step would be to obtain a reasonable appraisal as to the value of the business that the working child is inheriting. With your appraisal in hand, you would then be in a position to create monetary gifts in your Will to those of your children who are not inheriting the business. The monetary gifts would be designed to balance the value of the business interests which you are leaving to your working child. Before leaving this subject, we should point out that this is the type of matter which should be reviewed on an ongoing basis, because the value of the business at the time that you create your Will may be vastly different from the value of the business at the time of your death. If there is a radical difference between the two valuations, you might inadvertently create a serious disproportion between the value of the company that you are leaving to the working child, and the value of the gifts that you are leaving to your non-working children. When you are speaking to your lawyer, you may find that he may have many further recommendations to make, pertaining to a multitude of situations which could arise when you are contemplating leaving the business to your children. Certainly, he will have recommendations to make with respect to a situation where one of your children is a working shareholder and your other children are not. He is most likely to recommend a shareholders' agreement among such children. He is likely to recommend buy-sell arrangements and insurance arrangements and he is likely to make many other recommendations. As we previously indicated, a whole book can be devoted to succession planning when it comes to dealing with the family business, and the thoughts we have expressed are simply a summary of some of the issues that you might wish to think about.

LIVING SEPARATE AND APART

If you are living separate and apart from your spouse, and if you do not wish your separated spouse to inherit from your estate, it is important to review your existing Will to see whether that separated spouse is still named as a beneficiary in your Will, bearing in mind that separation is not equivalent to divorce. For this reason, if your separated spouse is named as a beneficiary in your Will, he or she will benefit from your Will once you pass away. If you wish to avoid this situation in circumstances where you are separated, it is extremely important to revise your Will or make a new one. Once you are divorced, your State law may revoke any gifts which you made to your former spouse in your Will.

Whether you are separated or divorced, it is important to review the names of the beneficiaries as they appear on any of your life insurance policies or retirement or pension plans. If your separated spouse, or, in the case of divorce, your former spouse, is named as a beneficiary in these documents, they are likely to benefit. You should be discussing these matters with your insurance representative and your lawyer if it is your wish to redesignate beneficiaries on these documents.

SECOND MARRIAGE PLANNING

You should always consider entering into a marriage contract when contemplating a second or subsequent marriage. Very often, this form of contract is known as a prenuptial agreement. Independent of that consideration, you may also want to consider whether you wish to have your new spouse as an executor in your Will. If you are concerned about conflict between your new spouse and the children of your first marriage, you may be deepening the conflict by naming your new spouse as executor in a Will that governs the benefits going to the children of your first marriage.

MAKING CHANGES TO YOUR WILL
A NEW WILL OR A CODICIL?

Provided that you have the mental capacity to do so, you can always revise your Will. You can choose to make a new Will which revokes the old one or you can choose to add to or subtract from your existing Will by way of a Codicil. Be conscious of the possibility of creating bad feelings when you wish to reduce the entitlement of one of your beneficiaries, or perhaps totally cut out that beneficiary. You might ask whether you should make a brand new Will in order to accomplish this purpose, or whether a simple Codicil to your existing Will is going to suffice.

Although a new Will will be more costly than a Codicil, in many cases we would recommend a new Will for the following reason. For example, if you use a Codicil to revise your Will in order to reduce a gift to your brother, or to cut him out entirely, you should be aware that when the documents are read after you die, both the Will and the Codicil are going to be read together. Those benefiting under your Will may see that you originally intended to benefit that particular brother, and then you changed your mind. If, on the other hand, you made a new Will, and assuming that your old Will was destroyed, no one would ever see what your original intentions were.

LIFE INSURANCE

Usually, you will name your spouse or child as your primary beneficiary under your life insurance policy. It is recommended, however, that you consult your insurance representative for the purpose of considering naming alternate beneficiaries on your policy, to address the situation which may arise if your primary beneficiary passes away before you do. Typically, one spouse will name the other spouse as primary beneficiary and the children as backup beneficiaries. When you pass away, the insurance company will send a check directly to the beneficiary, bypassing your estate.

There is a very important consequence to this type of arrangement. If the insurance money is going to your spouse or children, and is not going to your estate, the question then arises as to whether there will be enough money in your estate to pay its debts and taxes. If you fail to consider this issue, you may be creating animosity between the party who benefits from the proceeds of your life insurance policy, on the one hand, and the other beneficiaries of your estate. The one who takes the windfall, so to speak, under the life insurance policy, will not be subject to the burdens of your estate, which take the form of those debts and taxes. However, the other beneficiaries will be saddled with these burdens. Accordingly, you should consult your professional advisors on all of these issues so that you can avoid conflict among those who survive you. In some circumstances, this may mean that your advisors will recommend that you name your estate as beneficiary under your life insurance policies, as opposed to specifically named individuals. This arrangement would at least make money available to pay debts and taxes of your estate. This is a very personal consideration, but one which certainly must be addressed.

CONCLUSION

 Through our years of professional practice we have seen the erosion of family relationships, sometimes to the point of utter destruction of the family, for reasons which in many cases could have been avoided. Human emotion and sensitivity are such that it can take very little to commence driving a wedge between people who should really be loving each other, as opposed to bickering with each other. Just look at the photographs in your family album. Your daughter and your son running on the beach together; a family picnic or a family function, with warmth between brothers and sisters and parents and children. It is so tragic to examine evidence of such happiness, only to think that it can all be irretrievably destroyed. It does not take a sinister motive to create the damage. Destruction of your family can easily result from oversight, procrastination, trivialization of the real issues involved and disorganization itself. We are all in agreement on one thing. It is

absolutely impossible for you to express your wishes after you have become incapable, or after you have passed away. If you remember nothing else from reading this book, remember only this: do not presume that you will always be able to repair the misunderstandings that occur, as you can right now. Hopefully this book has given you the motivation to put the planning of your affairs on the front burner, to get professional advice, and to confront all of these matters so that you can avoid conflict within your family.

DISCLAIMER: The discussion contained in this presentation is not legal advice. Please consult your own professional advisor with respect to any steps you wish to carry out as a result of reading this book. For example, the laws governing the various topics which are discussed in this book will vary in some respects, depending upon which State you live in, or in which State your assets are located.